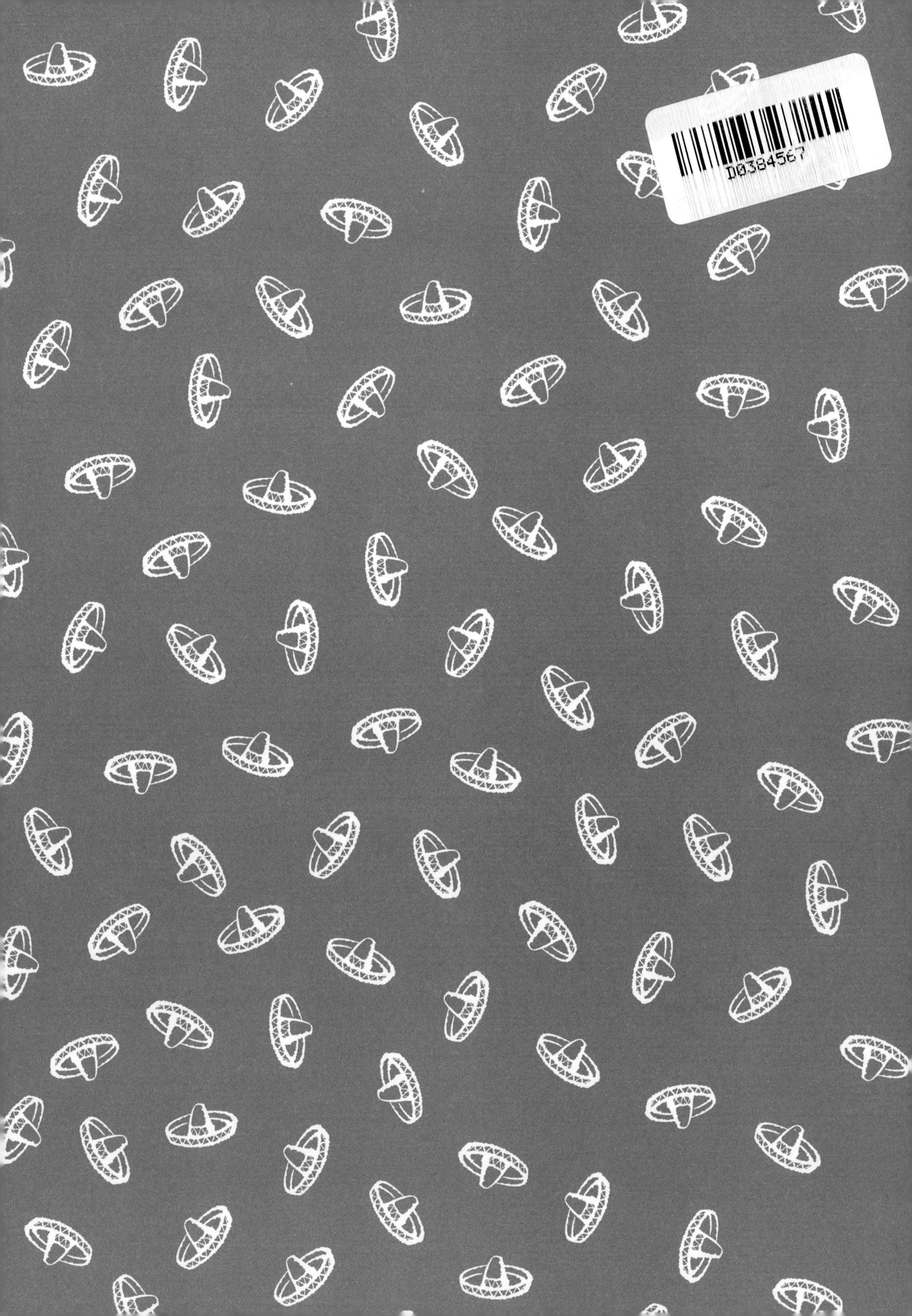

D0384567

MEXICO

CUISINES OF THE WORLD

MEXICO

JULIA FERNÁNDEZ

Food photography: Michael Brauner

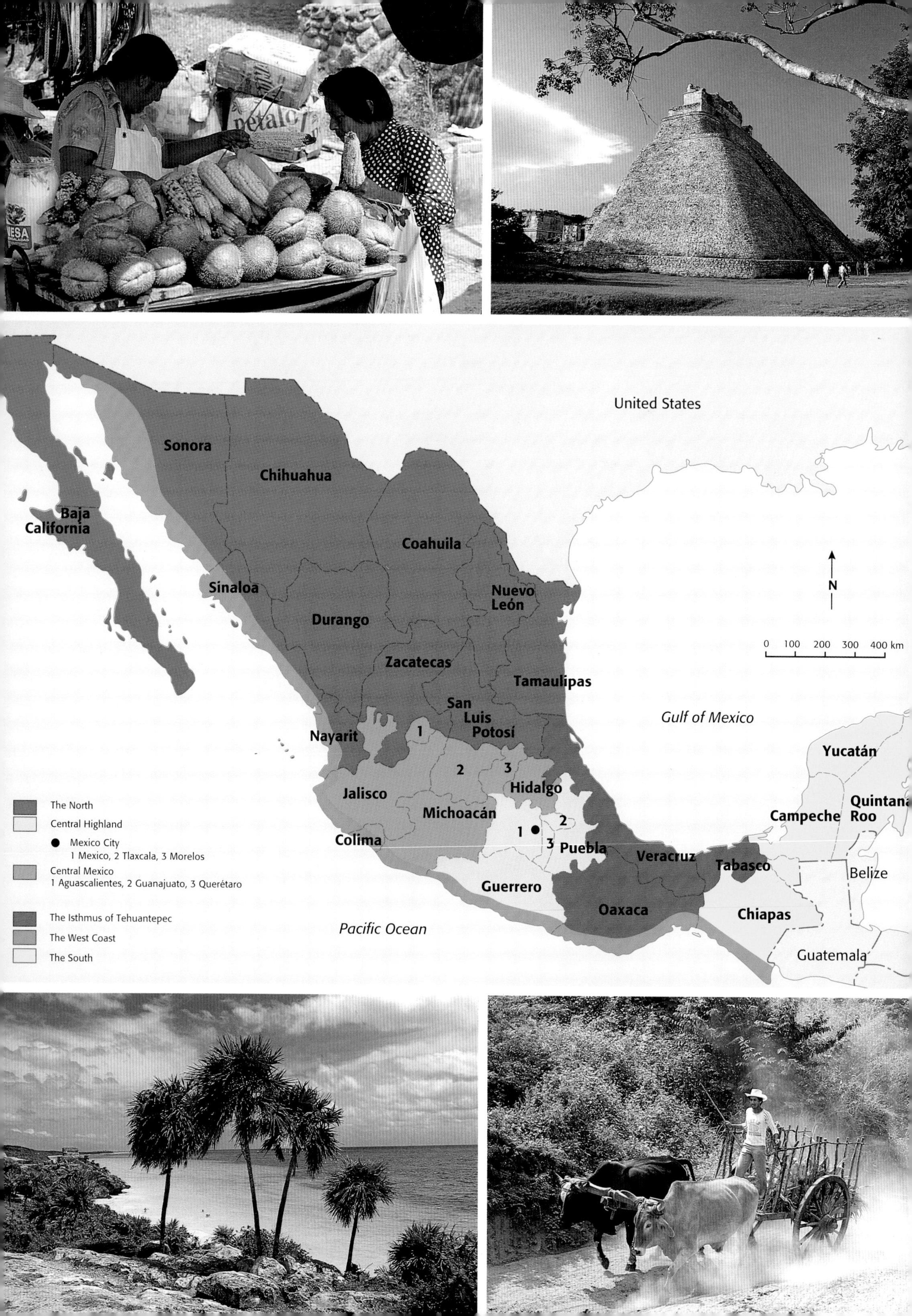

United States
Sonora
Chihuahua
Baja California
Coahuila
Sinaloa
Nuevo León
Durango
N
0 100 200 300 400 km
Zacatecas
Tamaulipas
San Luis Potosí
Gulf of Mexico
Nayarit
1
Yucatán
2
3
Hidalgo
Jalisco
Quintana Roo
Campeche
Michoacán
1
2
3
Colima
Puebla
Veracruz
Tabasco
Belize
Guerrero
Oaxaca
Chiapas
Pacific Ocean
Guatemala
The North
Central Highland
Mexico City
1 Mexico, 2 Tlaxcala, 3 Morelos
Central Mexico
1 Aguascalientes, 2 Guanajuato, 3 Querétaro
The Isthmus of Tehuantepec
The West Coast
The South

CONTENTS

MEXICO: A LAND OF STARK CONTRASTS

Since the Spaniards discovered Mexico in the early 16th century, this fascinating country has preserved its links with the Old World. Mexico is a land full of contrasts. Snow-covered volcanoes descend to barren deserts, in which cacti flourish

and cowboys herd cattle; idyllic tropical beaches and glamorous resorts that serve as playgrounds for the rich and famous; lush rainforests conceal mysterious ruins that provide tantalizing glimpses of sophisticated ancient cultures.

One of Mexico's great attractions is the Mexicans themselves, who will go out of their way to make a visitor feel welcome. They are not wealthy people, and for many life is far from easy, but nevertheless they laugh a great deal, despite, or maybe because of, their hardships, which are usually hidden from tourists behind the panorama of stunning scenery, picturesque markets, and riotous fiestas.

High on Mexico's central plateau, at the heart of what is the world's largest Spanish-speaking country, sits Mexico City, the country's capital. Here, at the numerous little food stalls – a feature of every Mexican town, large and small – it quickly becomes apparent that the locals enjoy eating outside the home. The vendors offer a variety of tasty tidbits, such as broiled corn-on-the-cob, and all kinds of tortillas. These thin pancakes – made from cornmeal or wheat flour, then filled, rolled, and broiled, baked, or fried – are served in many different ways, each with its own name. For the uninitiated, it takes a certain amount of expertise to decide whether you are being offered an enchilada, a burrito, or a quesadilla!

As with most Mexican food, the hot and spicy flavor comes from the ubiquitous chilies, the chili peppers, of which there some eighty different types, with varying degrees of fieriness. Fortunately, you do not have to go far in Mexico to find a drink to relieve the spiciness and quench your thirst at the same time. *Agua fresca*, a refreshing mix of fruit juice and water, is on sale at street stalls everywhere.

If you are lucky enough to be around for an authentic fiesta, you can indulge in all kinds of culinary delights. Best of all is to be invited to a private celebration, but even at the many public fiestas, held in the main square in the center of every town and village, there are lots of local delicacies to enjoy. The spectacle includes performances by the roving bands of street musicians, the mariachis, in their silver-buttoned suits and huge fanciful *sombreros*, who play and sing catchy songs. Dancing is in the blood, and on all these occasions young people in traditional costumes perform folk dances for an appreciative audience.

This book is designed to give an insight into the captivating and diverse land of Mexico and its imaginative cuisine. The first chapter provides an introduction to the regions, the people, their traditions, festivals, and cuisines. Then there are seven chapters of delicious, authentic dishes. Clear, step-by-step photographs illustrate some of the more complicated techniques, while variations, useful hints, and product information boxes complement the recipes, each of which is illustrated by a mouthwatering color photograph. A useful glossary of Mexican terms and ingredients, and a list of suggested menus to suit all occasions, round off the book. We hope you will have great fun cooking Mexican style. As the Mexicans say; *¡qué aproveche!* Enjoy your meal!

WORLDS OLD AND NEW

In Mexico city, if you stand in the Plaza de las Tres Culturas – Three Cultures Square – and take a look around, you will see the ruined remains of a great temple built by Mexico's original inhabitants, the Aztecs; a church in the Spanish colonial style; and a modern high-rise complex. Nowhere else is the relationship between Indian, Spanish, Mexican, and *mestizo* ("mixed blood") cultures, fundamental to an understanding of the Mexican psyche, so compellingly displayed.

This same combination of influences is also found in Mexican cuisine, which is a blend of the culinary heritage of the Old and New Worlds. Before the conquistadors invaded Mexico in 1519, the diet of the indigenous Indians was predominantly vegetarian, consisting of corn, potatoes, beans, squash, tomatoes, and chili peppers. Meat and fish were seldom eaten by these early civilizations, who bred only a few turkeys, and whose efforts at hunting and fishing brought only occasional success. It was the Spanish who introduced large-scale livestock rearing to Mexico, when they imported cattle, pigs, and poultry from their homeland as well as grains, fruits, spices, and cheese. Over the centuries, their own culinary traditions merged with those of the natives, resulting in a unique cuisine whose special charm is rooted in this fascinating cultural mix.

The country itself, which is bordered to the north by the United States, and to the south by Guatemala and Belize, is divided into 32 states which are loosely combined into a federation. The geography and topography vary enormously. Significant variations in climate create ideal conditions for cultivating a wide variety of agricultural produce.

In addition to these abundant agricultural treasures, there are the treasures of the sea. Cooks in Mexico's coastal areas prepare fish and seafood with particular inventiveness and finesse. Meat dishes are a specialty of northern Mexico; beef from the cattle reared on the high plains is of excellent quality. Fruit and vegetables are grown mainly in central Mexico; although the choice is wide, the dominant crops are beans and corn, both of which are traditional, native staple foods. The south yields an incredible variety of fruits – mangoes, pineapples, papayas, bananas, coconuts, guavas – the assortment is simply heavenly.

Even in pre-Columbian times, there was extensive trading between the regions in this rich and varied produce. The diversity of ingredients resulted in the creation of some highly imaginative dishes that are still enjoyed, not only in Mexico, but across the world.

With their varied produce arrayed before them, these street vendors make a colorful tableau before the imposing baroque cathedral on Mexico City's main square, the Zócalo.

Mexico City

In 1345, the Aztecs (also known as the Mexicas), a warring tribe from the north, arrived in the Valley of Mexico and settled on a swampy island in Lake Texcoco (now drained). Here, they founded the great city of Mexico-Tenochtitlan, capital of their empire and known to its earliest inhabitants as "the heart of the only world." The city thrived until 1521, when it finally succumbed to the might of Hernán Cortés and his force of Spanish soldiers, who set about destroying its fabulous monuments and building their own. Today, little is visible of the fabric of Tenochtitlan, and what remains lies buried beneath one of the largest cities in the world – Mexico City.

The Distrito Federal (D.F.), as the Mexicans call their capital, is situated at an altitude of 7,500 feet, in the high valley of Anahuác. On one of the (rare) clear days, the distant snow-covered peaks of Popocatépetl and Ixtaccihuatl are visible on the skyline. This vast city is, of course, the country's political and cultural heart, but it is also much more than that, for despite its turbulent past and ever-increasing problems with air pollution and overcrowding – at least 20 million people live here – it is a fascinating and pulsating city, full of life, color, and character.

The hub of the city is the Zócalo, second only in size to Moscow's Red Square, which is always thronged with newspaper, ice cream, and souvenir sellers, and colorful crowds. It is surrounded by many of the capital's most important monuments, including the baroque cathedral, the largest in Latin America, the huge Palacio Nacional, the seat of government, and the major government offices. Over the entrance hangs the Liberty Bell, a reminder of the war of independence against Spain which began on September 15, 1810 and continued for 11 years. Today, September 15 is a national holiday celebrated in style, like all Mexican fiestas. Just behind the cathedral stands the reconstructed base of the Templo Mayor, the great temple of the Aztecs.

The area surrounding the Zócalo, known as the Centro Histórico, has a wealth of splendid, noble palaces and baroque churches. The Palacio de Bellas Artes, a wonderful marble Art Nouveau building serving as both opera house and museum, offers an exhilarating weekly display of traditional folk dances, the Ballet Folklórico.

Other attractions include the Plaza Garibaldi, where many mariachis – Mexican street musicians – play in the evenings, and the Plaza de las Tres Culturas, where there is a plaque commemorating Cortes' defeat of the Aztecs on August 13, 1521. The commercial districts of the city, Zona Rosa and Polanco, are a busy mix of stores, luxury hotels, restaurants, bars, galleries, and nightclubs.

A typical Sunday treat for a Mexican family is an outing to the Xochimilco, "the place where the flowers grow," a labyrinth of canals and lakes situated in the southern part of the city. Here, families and groups of friends while away the afternoon gilding over the sparkling water in small, brightly decorated wooden flat-bottomed boats, rented by the hour and steered by boatmen. People bring their own picnics or buy food from the many floating snack bars, where broiled corn-on-the-cob, tortillas, and drinks are available. The convivial, carnival atmosphere is enhanced by the *mariachi* bands, which move from boat to boat, serenading as they go. A similarly colorful and exuberant atmosphere prevails in the many markets scattered all over the city, which owe much to Indian tradition. A particularly good one is La Merced, held on what was once the main market square. The atmosphere is one of bustle and color, with thousands of stalls selling vegetables and fruits from every part of the country. Separate sections are allocated to meat, poultry, and fish, and even to culinary and medicinal herbs – all very beautifully displayed. There are many charming little restaurants skirting the market, where you can sit at the counter or at an outdoor table enjoying a simple meal and watching life go by.

Although Mexico City has no unique culinary specialties of its own, it is famous for the variety and high standard of the food – of both national and international cuisines – on offer. The many inexpensive family-run restaurants in the city center are particular good value.

Resplendent in his elaborate Aztec headdress of exotic feathers, a dancer performs for the crowds in the Zócalo.

Gaily decorated flat-bottomed boats, their zinc awnings providing shade from the sun, ply the ancient, Aztec-made waterways of ochimilco.

A detail of the richly carved Pyramid of Quetzalcoatl, the serpent god, at Xochicalco, southwest of Mexico City.

Around Mexico City

Teotihuacan, the most awesome and well-known complex of ruins in Mexico lies 10 miles northeast of Mexico City. The country's largest archaeological site contains the Pyramids of the Sun and Moon which are 200 feet high, the Temple of Quetzalcoatl (the "Feathered Serpent"), with its fabulous sculptures and carvings, the Tepantitla Palace, and the magnificent Palace of the Jaguar. Reputedly the first city in the New World, Teotihuacan was in its heyday between 360 and 650 A.D., when it was the country's largest and most important trading center, with a population of circa 200,000. Why it so suddenly declined between 650 and 750 A.D. – and was subsequently abandoned – still remains a mystery. When the Aztecs, who set out from the north toward the Valley of Mexico in around 1200 A.D., discovered the ruined city, they revered it as a holy, mystical place created by the gods, and made pilgrimages there to worship.

At Tula, some 60 miles north of Mexico City in the state of Hidalgo, there are some equally fascinating remains. At the ceremonial center, on a hill, stands the Pyramid of the Morning Star, where visitors can marvel at the richly carved reliefs and the four colossal statues of warriors (*atlantes*) who once supported the temple roof.

Puebla, capital of the state of the same name, was founded by the Spaniards in 1531. It stands southeast of Mexico City, in a high, fertile valley whose setting contributes to its pleasantly cool mountain climate. An important industrial center, university town, and the head of a diocese, Puebla is a fine city that is well worth a visit, especially for its unspoiled historic center and brightly colored colonial buildings. The cathedral, the second largest in Mexico, is one of the country's loveliest religious buildings.

From a gastronomic point of view, Puebla holds a special appeal, for it is regarded as the cradle of Mexican cuisine. It is said that the nuns of the

The 18th-century spires of Santa Prisca, one of Mexico's finest churches, tower above the terra-cotta roofs of the colonial mining town of Taxco.

city's many convents were the first successfully to combine elements of Spanish and Indian cuisine. One of the most famous Mexican sauces, *mole poblano*, originated here, supposedly invented in the convent of Santa Rosa (now a museum of folk art). One version of the legend tells how the bishop once paid an unexpected visit to the convent. The nuns, naturally wanting to serve him something special, had no idea what to prepare. In desperation, they offered up a quick prayer, and then set about grinding every single ingredient they had in the larder to make into a sauce. The resulting concoction, inspired by divine intervention, was poured over the turkey and, with some trepidation, was set before their honored guest. God was clearly on the nuns' side, for the bishop was so delighted with the sauce that he immediately decreed it should become a national dish. The classic *mole poblano* – of which the significant ingredient is unsweetened chocolate – is still served with turkey or chicken, accompanied by tortillas, but there are several variations designed to complement other meats. Further delicacies to have emerged from Puebla's convent kitchens are *rompope*, a thick, creamy egg liqueur, and the candies known as *camotes*, made from sweet potato.

Taxco (pronounced Tasco), a romantic mining town preserved as a national monument, nestles in green hill country southwest of Mexico City. The outstanding feature of this little town of picturesque narrow streets and small white houses with red roofs is the exquisite baroque cathedral of Santa Prisca, built in the colonial style. Taxco is also known as "Silver City," for it is the center of the silver-mining industry and numerous silversmiths produce their wares in many local stores.

After a stroll around the town, visitors can relax on the terrace of one of the restaurants opposite the cathedral, perhaps sipping a *bertha*, a delicious mixture of lemonade and tequila. Other local specialties include *barbacoa*, mutton barbecued in leaves, and a dish that is rather less familiar to American palates – iguana stew! Semana Santa, Mexico's Holy Week, is marked nationwide by elaborate celebrations, but particularly in Taxco, where there are processions through the streets lasting late into the night, a moving and unmissable experience, if you have the stamina!

The church of Santo Domingo in Puebla, a jewel of Mexican baroque architecture, houses one of the country's most breathtakingly opulent chapels.

At a sleepy, ramshackle railroad station in Creel, Chihuahua, four men wait for a train to take them down the Copper Canyon. In this part of northern Mexico, where cattle ranches abound, jeans and cowboy hats are the typical attire.

The North

Vast herds of cattle, endless deserts, wheatfields, and bizarre cactus forests; the raucous yells of the *vaqueros*, echoing across the desolate landscape as they herd their cattle; moonlit nights spent beside a log fire with a feast of beans, beef, and tortillas, washed down with tequila – this is how many people imagine the life and landscape of northern Mexico.

Geographically, the region is difficult to define. It consists mainly of the vast states of Chihuahua, Coahuila, Durago, Nuevo León, and Tamaulipas; added to these are the Baja California peninsula, Sinaloa, and Sonora – although in aspect and character these three belong as much with those states along the Pacific coast as they do to the northern states.

The tracts of land that make up the Baja California peninsula, its shores lapped by the Pacific, are still barely accessible to tourists. However, for some years now it has been possible to take the "Mex 1" highway all the way from Tijuana in the north, at the U.S. border, right through to Cabo San Lucas in the south, a distance of around 1000 miles. The wild, barren landscape of deserts, cactuses, and mountains of the interior, separated from the mainland by the Gulf of California, is the perfect place for intrepid travelers and nature-lovers, or for those who simply want to get away from it all.

Thanks to modern irrigation techniques, the northern part of the peninsula has become Mexico's most important grape-growing region; it produces the pleasant and inexpensive table wines which are served throughout the country. The south is renowned for its idyllic beaches. One such resort, La Paz, capital of southern Baja, is linked by ferry to Los Mochis, on the other side of the Gulf of California in Sinaloa. This latter town is the starting point for one of Mexico's most fascinating and spectacular journeys, a 13-hour trip along the Chihuahua-Pacific Railway, passing through the remote Sierra Madre Occidental, through deep gorges and dense jungle, across sugar-cane fields, pastures full of grazing cattle, through wooded hills and the awesome Barranca del Cobre (Copper Canyon), to Chihuaha. It is an unforgettable experience.

In Chihuahua, Mexico's largest state – where the tiny breed of dog of the same name originated – many of the inhabitants are descended from German immigrants. One such group are the Mennonites. This austere Protestant sect makes a delicious cheese, shaped like a gigantic wheel, which is enjoyed throughout Mexico. *Queso menonito* is a good cheese for melting and a popular filling for the tortilla snack quesadillas.

The sweeping country of the north – Sonora, Coahuila, and Durango – is framed by the 1,500-mile-long Sierra Madre mountain ranges, the Occidental in the west and the Oriental in the east. Between them lie deserts interspersed with well-irrigated, intensely cultivated fertile plains, where the main crop is wheat. In this part of the world tortillas are made predominantly from wheat flour.

The cattle brought to the New World by the Spaniards quickly multiplied on the rolling grasslands of the north, resulting in the region's being noted today for its fine dairy produce. Cattle-breeding plays a major role in the national economy, and has had a strong influence on Mexican cuisine. The top-quality beef produced here is cut, salted, and dried in a unique way to make *cecina*, which is broiled or used to fill tortillas. Another dried and exquisitely seasoned meat is *machad*, which is often cut into thin strips and eaten with scrambled egg. In the east, where both the climate and the soil are too dry for rearing cattle, people generally keep goats, which require far less care. Spit-roasted kid, served with wheat tortillas and beans cooked in beer, is a popular dish in the industrial city of Monterrey, capital of Nuevo Léon.

At El Divisadero railway station, in the Sierre Madre, a Tarahumaran Indian woman deftly weaves a basket that will soon join the others on sale beside her.

The fishermen of Lake Patzcuaro still fish with traditional butterfly nets; their elegant geometric shapes make a stunning sight at sunset. In the background is Janitzio, the largest of the lake's seven islands.

Central Mexico

The 300-year period of Spanish rule, which lasted from 1521 until Mexican independence in 1821, had a strong formative influence on the towns and cities of the highlands of central Mexico – at times, here, you might almost believe your were in Spain. One such place is Guanajuato, in the state of the same name, which at its height was producing over half the world's silver. An important seat of learning since the Jesuits founded a university here in 1732, today it boasts a legacy of many fine buildings, among them a two-story covered market hall, built in 1910 by Gustave Eiffel, architect of the Eiffel Tower. The town was also the birthplace of the great muralist Diego de Rivera (1886–1957), examples of whose work can be seen at the house where he was born. Against a backdrop of narrow streets and tiny squares, an annual festival of theater and culture takes place here in October.

Guadalajara, capital of Jalisco in western central Mexico, is also strongly Spanish in character. It is the country's second largest city, yet with its colonial-style center it still retains the charm of a provincial town. The yellow domes of the cathedral on the main square glisten above the bay trees, under which the town's citizens enjoy leisurely Sunday strolls. Music from the mariachis, the professional bands of serenading musicians, echoes around the city squares, and you may be lucky enough to see a performance of the famous high-spirited Mexican Hat Dance. Among the city's cultural delights are its many 1930s murals by Clemento Orozco (1883–1949) displayed in the city hall and in the former orphanage. Mexico's largest covered market, the Mercado Libertad, can be found here. Among the wares on sale there is a range of skilfully crafted local folk art, such as pottery and leatherwork. The many small restaurants serve a varied selection of typical Mexican dishes. Guadalajara is the homeland of the charro, or Mexican cowboy. With their trademark broad-brimmed sombreros and magnificent, traditional costumes embroidered with silver, they make a spectacular sight at the charread, the Mexican version of a rodeo, held every Sunday. The proceedings are accompanied by much enthusiastic singing, and culminate in a parade that is well worth seeing. This region is also the site of one of Mexico's largest fiestas, held during October at the former Indian village of Zapopán, whose miraculous statue of the Virgin is carried through the town streets, accompanied by worshippers, bands, and dancers.

Not far from Guadalajara is Lake Chapala. In the many picturesque fishing villages lining its shores you might come across the little fried fish known as charalitos. Whether you are adventurous enough to sample the *gusanos de maguey*, or agave worms, whose crunchy texture is reminiscent of potato chips, is another matter. Those who are prepared to risk it usually wash them down with a shot of the tequila for which Jalisco is famous. This clear fiery spirit, produced in the small town of the same name from the fermented sap of the native agave or century plant, a type of cactus, is renowned far beyond the borders of Mexico.

Tourists flock to the state of Michoacán, with its diverse scenery of lakes, rivers, waterfalls, mountains, volcanoes, white sandy beaches, and the small, peaceful Lake Patzcuaro surrounded by mountains and forests. The fishing villages beside the lake are inhabited by members of the Tarascan tribes, who use butterfly nets to catch *blanquito*, a freshwater fish found only in these waters, which tastes particularly good fried in egg batter. Other popular attractions are the historic colonial buildings in Morelia, the beautiful state capital, and the nearby ruins of Tzintzuntzán, the old Tarascan capital.

In the middle of Lake Patzcuaro lies the island of Janitzio, famous for the celebrations that take place on the eve of the national festival of The Day of the Dead (November 12). On this night, villagers visit the graveyards to commune with departed spirits and to honor the dead with food, drink, and flowers. They stay by the gravesides until daybreak. This ritual dates back to the Aztecs, for whom death – in the form of regular human sacrifices of the gods – formed a necessary and intrinsic part of daily life. Latterday picnickers will consume quite a few bottles of wine during their remembrance feasts, the majority of it from the fertile valleys of Aguascalientes; this small state, north of Michoacán and Jalisco, produces some of Mexico's best wines.

Guadalajaran ranchers enjoy a charreada, the Mexican version of the rodeo; the older man wears traditional charro costume.

A grinning sugar skeleton, guitar in hand, adorns a window display during festivities for Mexico's Day of the Dead.

One of four colossal Olmec warrior heads in the Venta Museum Park, Villahermosa. The Olmecs, Central America's first urban civilization, were renowned for their fine sculpture.

The Isthmus of Tehuantepec

Mexico's central highlands are linked with the south by a narrow strip of land that at one point is only 125 miles wide from coast to coast. Here, the four states of Veracruz, Oaxaca, Tabasco, and the more southerly Chiapas, converge. Oaxaca, on the Pacific coast, is predominantly famous for its magnificent pre-Colombian ruins, the elaborate stone palaces of Mitla, set among cactuses, and Monte Albán, a vast ceremonial site of palaces, temples, pyramids, and tombs. Ancient civilizations flourished in this region, which is home today to more than 15 Indian tribes; the most famous of these are the Mixtecs and the Zapotecs, who once vied for power with one another before both groups were subjugated by the might of the warmongering Aztecs.

The state capital, Oaxaca, is an impressive city, dominated by fine colonial buildings, a baroque cathedral and the huge 16th-century monastery church of Santo Domingo. At the colorful, bustling Indian market held each Saturday, you can find black clay pottery and vividly colored textiles woven according to centuries-old traditions. On the last two Mondays in July, the city hosts one of the state's biggest fiestas – the Guelaguetza. During the celebrations, there are performances by folk-dancers in brightly colored costumes. A typical culinary specialty of the city is *mole negro*, an exquisite spicy sauce of chocolate, nuts, chili peppers, and other ingredients, traditionally served with chicken.

Stacking the shelves is an art in itself in this store in Oaxaca's city center, where tortillas, cheeses, and moles – spicy sauces – comprise the bulk of the goods on sale.

Veracruz and Tabasco, which meet on the coast of the Gulf of Mexico, are both centers of the oil industry. Despite the environmental pollution that affects many areas, there are still plenty of delights to attract the tourists. North of Jalapa, capital of Veracruz, and close to the idyllic little town of Papantla, stand the pre-Columbian ruins of El Tajín, with the magnificent seven-tiered Pyramid of the Niches rising amid fields of vanilla orchids (source of the fresh vanilla extract sold by local street vendors.) In Papantla, you may also be lucky enough to witness the ritual of the voladores, or flying pole dancers, whose gyrations were originally a fertility rite practiced by the Totonac Indians. Every Sunday, and on feast days, five voladores climb up to a tiny platform on top of a tall pole. There, four out of the five tie their ankles to ropes wound maypole-style around the pole. Then, while the fifth man plays a flute and beats a drum, the flyers hurl themselves from the platform and whirl slowly toward the ground as their ropes unwind. Further south, the busy and

flamboyant port of Veracruz, with its tropical panache and strong Afro-Caribbean atmosphere, has a very different feel from other Mexican cities. The inhabitants of Veracruz are renowned for their joie de vivre, vividly demonstrated during the city's riotous February carnival. Music fills the air, from African rhythms to calypso, and dancers and revelers throng the busy streets that are lit by the dazzling flares of endless fireworks.

A sight not to be missed in Tabasco's capital, Villahermosa, is the great stone heads carved by the legendary Olmecs (B.C. 1200–400), star attraction at the open-air Venta Museum Park. These colossal sculptures, the largest of which weighs around 40 tons, were brought here from the swampland site where they were first uncovered.

All along the coast you can enjoy a extraordinary range of fish dishes, among them *pescado a la veracruzana* (fish in a sauce of tomatoes, bell peppers, olives, and capers). The tasty huachinango a la veracruzana – red snapper cooked with garlic, spices, and chilis – is popular throughout Mexico.

This well-preserved row of houses – the only such street remaining in Veracruz – dates from the colonial period; it was near this city, Mexico's oldest and busiest port, that the Spanish conquistadors first landed in 1519.

A crescent of white towers fringes the deep blue waters of Acapulco Bay (right), once the exclusive haunt of the international jet set. Today, the idyllic beaches and unrivaled nightlife continue to attract visitors from all over the world.

The West Coast

Along the Pacific coast, palm-fringed bays and beaches of fine sand stretch for many miles beside a deep-blue, green-tinged sea, against a backdrop of towering cliffs – the whole resembling a very beautiful, picture postcard view. Popular activities here are fishing or water sports or you can simply relax under a palapa, a local sunshade made of palm leaves. It never gets unbearably hot, for the heat of the day is pleasantly tempered by a constant breeze. Hardly surprising that tourism in the region is booming!

Nine Mexican states border the west coast. Sonora and Sinaloa (which share many characteristics of the northern states), then Nayarit, Jalisco, Colima, Michoacán, Guerrero, which boasts the world-famous resort of Acapulco, Oaxaca, and Chiapas. One of the best-loved resorts along this stretch of coast is Mazatlán, in the northerly state of Sinaloa. This port, whose name means "place of deer," is famous for its beach, one of the longest and most beautiful on the Pacific, where serious fishermen from all over the world come to fish for marlin in the Sea of Cortes. It is also famous for its annual carnival, which is celebrated with particular fervor. Another very popular tourist spot is Puerto Vallarta, in Jalisco. Here, behind the luxury seafront hotels, lies a charming town of small white houses with red tiled roofs. To experience the luxurious lifestyle of these glamorous resorts at a more relaxed pace, try Las Hadas, an artificially created tourist center in mock-Moorish style, and Ixtapa, once a sleepy fishing village.

The most celebrated beach resort of the coast, and indeed of the whole of Mexico, is still Acapulco, whose very name has an air of exclusivity, a reputation largely established during the 1950s, when only the very wealthy could afford to holiday here. The

Two young women in traditional embroidered dress sell their pottery at a market in Colima.

Mexicans themselves tend to go to Acapulco not for the beaches but for the sophisticated nightclubs and the shows. In the town's many discos and bars, the action begins at 11 p.m. and seldom ends much before sunrise. One thrilling spectacle is provided nightly by the daredevil *clavadistas* who earn a few pesos from the crowd, by diving off the 133-foot-high cliffs into the narrow cove of La Quebrada.

Fresh fish is a mainstay of the diet of all the coastal states, and this 930-mile-long stretch of coast is no exception. The favorite fish for making *ceviche*, raw fish marinated with tomatoes and cilantro, is the sierra fish a kind of tuna renowned for its superb flavor. There are also many kinds of seafood, which are either simply broiled or served with a variety of exquisite sauces. As one might expect, the freshest, best dishes – and those most representative of local cuisine, are found not in the tourist resorts but in the fishing villages, or at the primitive beachside huts that are found all along the coast.

There is a heavenly selection of tropical fruit in this region, especially mangoes and pineapples, which are used as inexpensive thirst-quenchers on the beach. Coconuts, too, are plentiful; in Colima, the vast plantations stretch right down to the sea. Coconut is used to make exotic drinks and desserts, such as the popular *cocada*.

When visiting these western states, it is certainly worthwhile traveling inland to visit the less well-known and quieter rural areas, where you will find many charming little towns with their own colorful markets and small, authentic restaurants.

Gaily decorated tombs are a characteristic feature of Mayan cemeteries in the north of Yucatán.

The South

Many people regard the south as the most beautiful part of Mexico. It is principally famous as the home of the magnificent ruins of the unique Mayan culture. Together with the Aztecs and the Incas (in Peru and Bolivia), the Mayas were the most important early colonizers of Latin America. Fine examples of their highly sophisticated architecture are found all over the region. They include the pyramids and temples of Palenque, in Chiapas, and, in the north, the sites of Chichén Itzá and Uxmal, undoubted high points of a visit to the peninsula.

The capital of the Yucatán is Mérida. Founded on the site of a Mayan city in 1542, it was once known as the "White City," on account of its whitewashed houses and general cleanliness. Today, it is the predominantly white clothing of its inhabitants that is most conspicuous; the white dresses of the women, embroidered with brightly colored flowers, are particularly striking. The people here speak Maya quiché, the ancient, very musical, language of their forebears. The handmade wall-hangings made from sisal, a stiff fiber derived from the fleshy leaves of the Mexican agave plant, also the source of tequila, are a local specialty.

A large part of southern Mexico is occupied by the state of Chiapas, which has close historical and cultural links with Guatemala. Scenically, Chiapas is the country's most diverse region, with its unspoilt rainforests, lakes, rivers, volcanoes, waterfalls, and coasts. Its leading attractions include the enchanting ruined palaces of the Mayan cities of Bonampak and Yaxchilián, situated in the heart of the rainforest and accessible only by boat or light aircraft. In Chiapas, the descendents of the Mayas continue to wear traditional costume, in this case, black with colorful embroidery. The men sport distinctive wide flat hats, sometimes adorned with ribbons.

San Cristobal de las Casas, also in Chiapas, is a lively, picturesque town famous for its market, one of the most colorful in Mexico. In this part of the world, many of the old barter traditions still survive, and brightly colored vegetables and sweet-scented herbs are exchanged for beautiful textiles and embroidery.

The Yucatán peninsula, pushing out into the Gulf of Mexico, encompasses the states of Campeche, Yucatán and Quintana Roo. In addition to great relics of Mayan civilization, these states boast beaches of dazzling white sand, and clear, turquoise-blue waters that make a diver's paradise. In the early morning at the large fishing port of Ciudad del Carmen, in western Campeche, you can watch fishermen bringing in their splendid catch – baskets of squid, octopus, sea bass, red snapper, and *cazón*, a small dogfish regarded throughout the region as a delicacy. The port is also a shrimping center, and these crustaceans feature largely on local menus.

Cancún – its name means "crock of gold" – was once a sleepy fishing village on an offshore lagoon in the state of Quintana Roo. The last quarter of the 20th century, saw it transformed into a sophisticated tourist center, with long sandy beaches, luxury hotels, and a fantastic range of opportunities for water sports enthusiasts. If a quieter and more authentically Mexican atmosphere is what you are looking for, then the islands of Mujeres and Cozumel are the places to visit.

Southern Mexico has a number of its own culinary specialties. The tamales, which in other parts of the country are wrapped in corn husks, are prepared here in fresh banana leaves; another Yucatán dish is *cochinita pibil*, spicy pork wrapped in banana leaves and cooked in an underground oven. Be very careful with salsas: southern cooks often use the tiny, flame-red and searingly hot chili habanero, whose fieriness can only be relieved by quantities of bread, bananas, and beer!

Mexican beer, as well as being consumed in large quantities by the Mexicans themselves, is exported worldwide. Delicious, and relatively low in alcohol, it is available in both dark (*oscura*) and light (*clara*) varieties, and is an excellent accompaniment to all Mexican food.

A young Mayan girl, in front of her hut in the little village of Muma in Yucatán, smiles shyly at the camera. She wears the traditional white embroidered huipil.

At the ruins of the Pyramid of Kukulcán at Chichén Itzá, a chacmool solemnly stands guard in front of the Temple of the Warriors.

TORTILLAS, TACOS, AND TAMALES

Tortillas have come to symbolize Mexican cooking since they are served at practically every meal. As well as being delicious, these fresh, warm pancakes serve a practical purpose, for they are often used instead of a spoon or plate.

There are a number of different versions of tortilla, which can make reading a menu, or a recipe book, very confusing if you are not familiar with them. As a brief guide: tacos are soft, filled, rolled-up tortillas. If they are-then fried, they are called flautas. Those that are filled with meat or vegetables are called burritos. Quesadillas are filled, folded in half, and fried. Crisply fried tortillas spread with beans and sprinkled with strips of meat, vegetables, and cheese, are known as tostadas. Enchiladas are tortillas spread with sauce, fried, filled, and rolled. Totopos are small, crisp pieces of tortilla used for dipping. Tamales are made of tortilla dough, *masa harina*, filled, wrapped in corn husks, and steamed.

Corn tortillas are made from *masa harina*, corn soaked in slaked lime, then ground coarsely. In the north of the country tortillas are prepared with wheat flour. The cornmeal is mixed with water to make the *masa*, or dough, which is then shaped into individual tortillas and fried on a special griddle called a *comal*. Shaping tortillas by hand is a tricky operation, this recipe shows you how to do it without a tortilla press.

Cornmeal Tortillas

Tortillas de maíz

Can be made in advance • All regions

Makes 8 tortillas

1 ⅓ cups yellow or white cornmeal
½ tsp. salt

Preparation time: 45 minutes

67 cal. per tortilla

1 Place the cornmeal and salt in a mixing bowl. Slowly add ¾ cup lukewarm water, stirring constantly with the pastry hook attachment of a hand mixer, or a wooden spoon, to make a smooth, moist dough. Cover the bowl and leave to stand for about 15 minutes.

2 Cut out two squares of nonstick baking paper about 8 inches square. Divide the dough into eight equal-sized pieces. Heat a nonstick skillet without fat.

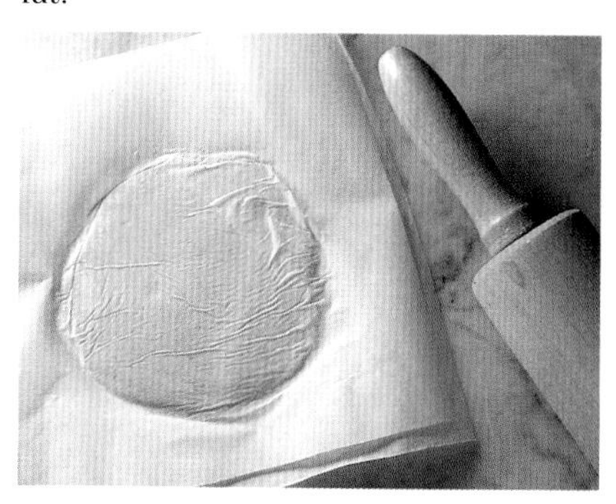

3 Take one portion of dough, place it between the two sheets of paper, and roll it out to a circle about 5 inches in diameter (*above*). It is best to roll out the tortillas one at a time and then

cook them. Do not roll them all at once, otherwise the paper will become damp and flabby and it will be impossible to peel it away from the dough.

4 Immediately peel off the top sheet of paper. Place the tortilla in the heated skillet, paper side upward, and remove the paper (below left). Cook the tortilla over medium heat for 30 to 60 seconds on each side, until dark spots develop. Remove from the pan and keep warm.

Variation: For a very quick dough, mix 1 cup cornmeal, 1 cup all-purpose flour, 1 tsp. salt and 1½ –2 cups lukewarm water to a soft dough. Cover and leave to stand for 20 minutes. Shape the dough into eight equal-sized balls. On a lightly floured surface, roll them into very thin circles about 6 inches in diameter. Cook the tortillas one at a time in a dry, nonstick pan for about 1 minute on each side.

Note: In Mexico, the traditional dough used to make tortillas is called *masa*. To make masa, dried grains of corn are first soaked in a slaked lime-and-water solution, then they are husked and ground. *Masa harina* (also known as maize flour) is all-purpose flour made from dried masa; it is available from all Mexican stores and supermarkets in Mexican neighborhoods.

This recipe uses yellow cornmeal with exactly the right quantity of water added to make the cooked tortillas easy to roll. If you want to use *masa harina*, prepare the dough as described, using 2 tsp. vegetable oil or lard, 1 cup *masa harina* and 2 cups tepid water. Cooked tortillas will keep for one or two days in the refrigerator, wrapped in plastic wrap.

Alternatively, you can buy ready-made, vacuum-packed tortillas but homemade ones will always taste better.

Wheat Tortillas

Simple • Northern Mexico

Tortillas de harina

makes 8 tortillas

Makes 8 tortillas
1 ½ cups all-purpose flour
1 tsp. salt

Preparation time: 45 minutes

74 cal. per tortilla

1 Place the all-purpose flour and salt in a mixing bowl. Slowly stir in 7 tbsp. lukewarm water. Mix well.

2 Knead the dough with your hands until it is smooth and comes away from the sides of the bowl. Cover and leave to stand for about 15 minutes.

3 Divide the tortilla dough into eight equal-sized pieces. On a lightly floured surface, roll out each piece to a thin circle about 6 inches in diameter.

4 Heat a nonstick skillet without fat and fry the tortillas one at a time over medium heat for about 1 minute on each side. If the tortillas start to form bubbles, press them gently onto the base of the skillet with a metal spatula, so that they cook evenly on both sides.

5 The tortillas are ready when they develop brown flecks. Place the cooked tortillas in a basket lined with napkins to keep them warm while cooking the remainder.

Note: Tortillas are so easy to make it is worth making a large batch and then freezing some of them. They can be served in place of bread with many different kinds of dishes.

Tacos with Beef Filling

Takes time • Northern Mexico

Tacos con relleno de carne de res

Makes 8 tacos

1 cup beef broth
13 oz. fillet of beef
salt • vegetable oil for frying
8 cooked wheat tortillas (see opposite)
8 large lettuce leaves
8 tbsp. red bean sauce (see page 54)
2 small beefsteak tomatoes
8 tbsp. sour cream
8 tbsp. Mexican salsa (see page 54)
7 tbsp. Jack cheese

Preparation time: 1 hour (plus 45 minutes for the tortillas and 40 minutes for the red bean sauce and Mexican salsa)

290 cal. per taco

1 Bring the broth to a boil in a small saucepan. Add the beef, cover the pan, and simmer gently over medium heat for about 30 minutes, or until cooked.

2 Remove the meat from the broth, allow to cool, then either tear or chop it into small pieces, and season lightly with salt.

3 Heat a little oil in a skillet, and sauté the tortillas, one at a time, in the hot oil to soften them. Remove them from the pan and lay them out in a single layer on a work surface.

4 Wash the lettuce leaves and shake them dry. Spread the red bean sauce over the tortillas. Arrange the lettuce leaves on top, then the chopped meat.

5 Wash and halve the beefsteak tomatoes and chop into small dice. Arrange the diced tomatoes on top of the tortillas. Top each tortilla with 1 tbsp. sour cream and 1 tbsp. Mexican salsa.

6 Coarsely grate the cheese straight over the tortillas. Roll them up and serve immediately.

Note: The two sauces can be made in advance, if wished. They will keep in the refrigerator for three to four days.

Cheese Enchiladas

Enchiladas de queso

Quick • All regions

Makes 8 enchiladas

1 ¾ cups cream cheese
7 tbsp. shredded Jack or Cheddar cheese
4 green onions (scallions)
1 tsp. dried oregano
salt • freshly ground white pepper
vegetable oil for frying
8 cooked cornmeal tortillas (see page 26)
green tomato sauce (see page 58)
lettuce leaves and tomato wedges for garnish (optional)

Preparation time: 35 minutes (plus 45 minutes for making the tortillas and 35 minutes for the tomato sauce)

170 cal. per enchilada

1 Mix the cream cheese and 4 tbsp. of the cheese in a bowl. Trim and wash the green onions (scallions), cut them into thin rings, and stir into the cheese. Season with oregano, salt, and pepper.

2 Preheat the oven to 425° F. Heat the oil in a skillet and briefly sauté the cooked tortillas, one at a time, in the hot oil to soften them. Transfer them to a plate.

3 Grease an ovenproof baking dish. Spread the tortillas with green tomato sauce. Take half the cheese mixture and spread some over each tortilla. Roll up the tortillas and arrange them in the baking dish. Top with the rest of the cheese mixture, then sprinkle the remaining shredded cheese over the top of them.

4 Bake in the center of the oven for 15 to 20 minutes, or until the cheese on the top is lightly browned. Serve with lettuce cut into strips, and tomato wedges, if wished.

Variation: Cook 2 chicken breast fillets and cut them into small pieces. Finely chop 4 green onions (scallions). To make the filling, mix the chicken and green onions (scallions) with the 4 tbsp. chopped cilantro and 2 crushed garlic cloves. Pour Mexican salsa (see page 54) over the cooked tortillas.

Burritos with Vegetables

Burritos de verduras

Easy • Central Mexico

Serves 4

1 small onion • 1 carrot
vegetable oil for frying
2 garlic cloves • 1 small zucchini
1 small red bell pepper
2 tsp. chili powder
1 tsp. ground cumin
1 tsp. dried oregano
salt • freshly ground black pepper
⅔ cup canned corn, drained
1 cup canned red kidney beans, drained
8 cooked wheat tortillas (see page 28)

Preparation time: 45 minutes (plus 45 minutes for the tortillas)

450 cal. per portion

1 Peel and finely chop the onion. Peel and coarsely grate the carrot. Heat 2 tbsp. oil in a large skillet and fry the onion and carrot over low heat for about 5 minutes. Peel and crush the garlic and add to the pan.

2 Wash the zucchini, top-and-tail it, then cut it first into ¼ inch slices and then into small dice.

3 Cut the pepper in half lengthwise, then trim and wash it. Cut first into strips, then into small dice.

4 Add the diced pepper and zucchini to the sautéed vegetables in the pan. Season with the chili powder, cumin, oregano, salt, and pepper, then cover the pan and cook the vegetables over low heat for about 5 minutes.

5 Place the sweetcorn and the kidney beans in a sieve and rinse under cold running water, then drain. Stir them into the vegetables in the pan and then cook, covered, for a further 10 minutes.

6 Heat more oil in a skillet and briefly turn the tortillas, one at a time, in the hot oil to soften them.

7 Spread the filling over the tortillas, roll them up, and serve immediately.

Note: Burritos taste good served with guacamole (see page 57), fine strips of lettuce, and chopped tomatoes.

Chicken Tostadas

Easy • Michoacán

Tostadas de pollo

Serves 4

2 onions
4 garlic cloves
1 ¼ lb. chicken breast fillets
1 ¾ cups chicken broth
2 ¼ lb. beefsteak tomatoes
1 jalapeño pepper (see Glossary)
1 small bunch fresh cilantro or flat-leaved parsley (about 2 oz.)
salt
freshly ground black pepper
vegetable oil for frying
8 cooked cornmeal tortillas (see page 26)
8 large lettuce leaves
7 tbsp. sour cream
½ cup feta or fresh white Mexican cheese

Preparation time: 1 hour (plus 45 minutes for the tortillas)

480 cal. per portion

1 Peel the onions and garlic. Cut one of the onions in half and place one half in a saucepan with 1 garlic clove and the chicken breast fillets. Add the chicken broth, bring slowly to a boil, then cover and cook over medium heat for 25 to 30 minutes. Remove the chicken from the pan and leave to cool.

2 Meanwhile, plunge the tomatoes into boiling water, and remove the skins and seeds. Wash the chili pepper and deseed it.

3 Put the chili pepper, tomatoes, and the remaining onions and garlic in a food processor or blender and grind them together. Wash the cilantro or parsley and shake dry. Finely chop the leaves and stir them into the tomato sauce. Season with salt and pepper.

4 Finely chop the chicken breast; set aside. Heat the oil in a skillet and sauté the tortillas, one at a time, in the hot oil to soften them.

5 Spread half the tomato sauce over the tortillas. Wash and dry the lettuce leaves and arrange them on top of the tortillas. Top the tortillas with equal portions of chicken and pour the rest of the tomato sauce over the top.

6 Add a dollop of sour cream to each tortilla, and coarsely grate or crumble the cheese on top. Place two tostadas on each individual plate and serve at once so they do not go soggy.

Drink: Tequila goes particularly well with these delicious tostadas.

Oven-baked Tortillas

Takes time • Sonora

Chimichangas al horno

Makes 8 tortillas

1 lb. 5 oz. bladebone pork roast
2 tbsp. clarified butter (see Glossary)
2 tbsp. white wine vinegar
1 garlic clove
1 fresh poblano chili pepper (see Glossary)
½ tsp. dried oregano
½ tsp. ground cumin • salt
vegetable oil for frying
8 cooked wheat tortillas (see page 28)
Mexican salsa (see page 54)
⅔ cup sour cream
4 tbsp. freshly grated queso añejo (see Glossary), or Parmesan

Preparation time: 1 hour (plus 45 minutes for the tortillas and 20 minutes for the salsa)

400 cal. per portion

1 Chop the pork into very small dice. Heat the clarified butter in a skillet and fry the meat, in batches, over high heat for about 5 minutes, or until it is crisp and brown.

2 Add the vinegar. Peel and crush the garlic and add to the meat. Wash and deseed the chili pepper. Add to the meat and season with oregano, cumin, and salt. Cover and simmer over low heat for about 10 minutes.

3 Heat the oil in a skillet and turn the tortillas, one at a time, in the hot oil to soften them. Preheat the oven to 400 degrees.

4 Spread Mexican salsa over each tortilla and top with meat filling, then fold the tortillas in half.

5 Mix the sour cream and cheese in a bowl. Arrange the folded tortillas in a greased baking pan and pour the cheese sauce over the top.

6 Bake in the center of the oven for 15 minutes. Serve straight from the baking pan.

Note: You can use different sauces, such as green tomato sauce (see page 58) or devil sauce (see page 57), if preferred.

Pork Tamales

Hearty • Central Mexico

Tamales de cerdo

Serves 4

20 dried corn husks (see Note)
1 lb. 2 oz. masa harina (see Glossary)
1 cup beef broth
6 tbsp. lard
salt
1 medium-sized onion
1 pound 5 oz. pork tenderloin
2 tbsp. vegetable oil
3 garlic cloves
2 fresh medium-hot chili peppers (see Glossary)
1 can tomatillos (see Glossary), about 1 ½ cups, drained
1 small bunch fresh cilantro or flat-leaved parsley

To serve:
Devil sauce (see page 57)

Preparation time: 1 hour (plus 3 hours soaking time and 1 hour cooking time)

266 cal. per portion

1 Place the corn husks in a bowl, pour enough warm water over them to cover, and leave to soak for about 3 hours.

2 Meanwhile, place the masa harina in a bowl with the broth. Using the dough hook attachment of a hand mixer, knead this mixture to a thick dough. Melt the lard and add to the dough with a little sat, and continue to knead for a good 5 minutes. Cover the dough and set aside.

3 Peel and finely chop the onion. Slice the pork into narrow strips. Heat the oil in a skillet and fry the meat in batches over high heat for about 5 minutes, until well browned, then remove from the pan.

4 Fry the onion in the remaining fat over medium heat until soft. Peel and crush the garlic and add to the onion. Wash the chili peppers, discard the seeds, and cut the chilies into thin rings. Briefly fry the chili rings with the rest of the vegetables.

5 Strain the tomatillos through a sieve and add them to the vegetables in the pan. Cover and cook for 5 minutes, then grind the vegetables in a blender.

6 Simmer the purée, uncovered, in a saucepan for about 10 minutes, until reduced and thickened.

7 Wash the fresh cilantro or parsley, shake dry and coarsely chop the leaves. Stir the meat strips and the chopped leaves into the vegetable purée

.

8 Pat one corn husk dry. Spread it out and place 1 ½ tbsp. dough in the middle of the husk; press it down flat, leaving a wide border of husk. Place 1½ tbsp. filling on top of the dough (*above*).

9 Roll up the corn husk, starting at the long edge. Press the husk to flatten it slightly and then fold over the ends (*above*). Repeat to make 16 tamales.

10 Fill two large saucepans with water to a depth of about 2 inches. Bring to a boil, then reduce the heat. Line two steamers with two corn husks each and place one over each pan.

11 Place half the tamales in each steamer, laying them close together at a slight angle. Cover and steam over medium heat for 1 hour, or until the husk comes away easily from the dough. Serve with a small bowl of Devil Sauce.

Note: Dried corn husks are available from specialty food stores; if you cannot find them, use 8-inch squares of aluminum foil to make the packages.

Mushroom Quesadillas

Takes time • All regions

Quesadillas de hongos

Serves 4

cornmeal tortilla dough (see page 26)
1 small onion • 6 garlic cloves
7 tbsp. olive oil • 4 cups mushrooms
4 fresh epazote or lemon balm leaves (see page 69)
salt • chili powder

To serve:
lime slices and Mexican salsa (see page 54)

Preparation time: 20 minutes (plus 35 minutes for the tortilla dough)

160 cal. per quesadilla

1 Shape the tortilla dough into eight equal-sized balls. Cover with plastic wrap and set aside.

2 Peel and finely chop the onion. Peel and crush the garlic. Heat 2 tbsp. of the oil in a skillet and sauté the onion until soft, then add the garlic.

3 Trim and rinse the mushrooms, slice thinly, then chop coarsely. Add them to the onion and garlic, and cook over medium heat until most of the liquid in the pan has evaporated.

4 Briefly wash the epazote or lemon balm leaves, shake dry, chop finely, and stir into the mushrooms. Season with salt and a little chili powder.

5 On a lightly floured surface, roll out the eight balls of tortilla dough (see Steps 2 and 3 on page 26) to make circles about 18 inches in diameter. They should be slightly thicker than the usual tortillas. Spoon the filling onto one half of each circle, then fold over the other half to make a semicircle, and press the edges firmly together.

6 Heat the remaining oil in a deep skillet and fry the quesadillas for about 3 minutes on each side, until golden-brown. Garnish with the lime slices, and serve with Mexican salsa.

Variation: Cheese quesadillas
(Quesadillas de queso)
Mix together 7 tbsp. freshly grated Parmesan cheese, 1 egg, 2 tbsp. milk and 1 chopped sprig of epazote or lemon balm, and season with salt and pepper. Fill the quesadillas with this mixture and fry as described above.

Red Chilaquiles

Simple • All regions

Chilaquiles rojos

Serves 4

1 lb. 12 oz. ripe beefsteak tomatoes
3 canned jalapeño peppers or 1 fresh hot chili pepper (see Glossary)
1 large onion
4 garlic cloves
4 tbsp. vegetable oil
salt
1 ½ cups chicken broth
1 lb. 2 oz. chicken breast fillets
12 cooked cornmeal tortillas (see page 26)
1 small bunch fresh cilantro (about 1 oz.)
4 tbsp. sour cream
2 tbsp. crumbled feta or queso menonito

Preparation time: 1 hour (plus 45 minutes for making the tortillas)

570 cal. per portion

1 Plunge the tomatoes into boiling water, remove the skins and seeds, and coarsely chop the flesh. Wash the chili peppers, discard the seeds, and finely chop the chilies.

2 Peel and finely chop the onion. Peel and crush the garlic. Heat 1 tbsp. of the oil in a saucepan and sauté the onion for 2 to 3 minutes, then add the garlic and cook for a further 1 minute. Stir in the tomatoes and chili peppers, then season with salt. Simmer over low heat for about 10 minutes.

3 Purée the vegetable mixture in a food processor or blender and return the purée to the pan. Heat the chicken broth in a saucepan, add the chicken breasts, cover, and cook over low heat for about 30 minutes. Remove the chicken and cut it into narrow strips. Add the chicken broth to the vegetable purée, and cook until the sauce is heated through.

4 Cut each tortilla into eight pieces. Heat the remaining oil in a skillet and sauté the tortilla pieces for about 5 minutes, or until crisp.

5 Wash and finely chop the cilantro. Carefully stir the cilantro, tortilla chips, and chicken into the tomato sauce. Spread the sour cream and the crumbled cheese on top. Cover the pan and cook for 6 to 8 minutes, or until the cheese starts to melt.

Note: This dish can also be made with *tomatillos* (green tomatoes), in which case it is called *chilaquiles verdes*.

SALADS, EGGS, AND LIGHT MEALS

Salads are one of the glories of Mexican cuisine, and are served not as side dishes but as a separate course in their own right, often as the appetizer, as in California. Mexico has an abundance of fresh fruits, so fruit salads are a common breakfast dish, as well as being available all day long at the many street food stalls. Salads made with exotic fruits are often seasoned with hot spices, which for American palates may take some getting used to, but the mixture of flavors is fascinating. Other popular salad ingredients include avocados, tomatoes, chili peppers, onions, and radishes. Different types of fish and seafood are also prepared as salads, and are especially delicious when served chilled on hot days.

Mexicans are very partial to eggs, which for breakfast they like scrambled with onion, tomatoes, and chili pepper (*huevos a la mexicana*). Another favorite is *huevos rancheros* (rancher-style eggs), tortillas topped with fried eggs, tomatoes, and chili peppers. There are innumerable variations on egg dishes. In Veracruz, eggs are served with red kidney beans, in Mexico City with spicy chorizo sausage, and in Puebla they are mixed with tomato sauce, chili peppers, and heavy cream, topped with cheese, and browned in the oven perfect snack dish for any time of day.

Avocado Salad

Easy • Michoacàn

Ensalada de aguacate

Serves 4

2 large beefsteak tomatoes (about 14 oz.)
2 ripe avocados
juice of 1 lemon
4 green onions (scallions)
5 radishes
6 slices bacon
2 tbsp. vegetable oil
3 tbsp. white wine vinegar
cayenne pepper
sugar
salt
freshly ground black pepper

Preparation time: 30 minutes

550 cal. per portion

1 Plunge the tomatoes into boiling water, remove the skins, and cut each one into eight wedges, discarding the hard flesh under the stalk.

2 Peel the avocados, cut them in half lengthwise, and pit them. Cut the flesh crosswise into thin slices. Sprinkle immediately with lemon juice to prevent it discoloring.

3 Trim and wash the green onions (scallions) and cut them into thin rings. Trim, wash, and thinly slice the radishes. Arrange all the vegetables attractively in rows on four individual plates.

4 Cut the bacon slices into narrow strips. Heat the oil in a skillet and fry the bacon slowly over medium heat until the fat runs. Remove the bacon strips from the pan and drain them on paper towels.

5 Pour the white wine vinegar into the fat remaining in the pan. Add a little cayenne pepper and sugar, and season with salt and pepper.

6 Bring briefly to a boil, then pour the hot dressing over the salad on the plates. Sprinkle the strips of bacon over the top, and serve at once.

Avocados

This green, pear-shaped fruit was called *ahua quatl*, meaning "butter of the forest," by the Aztecs, a particularly appropriate name since, when ripe, the yellowish-green flesh is very creamy. There are more than 400 varieties of avocado, some with dark knobbly skin, others with a smooth, shiny green skin.

Avocados are picked while still firm, so that they will not bruise during shipping. The creamy texture and characteristic flavor will only develop when the fruit is fully ripe, which is when the flesh gives slightly when gently pressed. They are used mostly in savory dishes, often as an appetizer or in a salad, or in dips such as the tasty Mexican guacamole.

To open an avocado, cut it in half lengthwise and twist the halves in opposite directions until they separate. Sprinkle the cut surfaces immediately with lemon or lime juice, to prevent the flesh from discoloring when it comes into contact with the air.

Ripe avocados will keep for two to three days if stored in the refrigerator. Unripe ones will ripen if they are kept at room temperature for two or three days, wrapped in newspaper.

Pineapple and Papaya Salad

Quick and easy • Veracruz

Ensalada de frutas

Serves 4

1 medium-sized fresh pineapple
1 large ripe papaya
1 fresh medium-hot chili pepper (see Glossary)
small bunch fresh cilantro or flat-leaved parsley (about ½ oz.)
1 lemon
salt

Preparation time: 20 minutes

93 cal. per portion

1 Peel the pineapple carefully, cutting off all the leaves. Cut the pineapple lengthwise into four pieces and discard the hard core. Chop the flesh into 1-inch chunks and place them in a bowl.

2 Peel the papaya, then cut it in half lengthwise and scoop out the seeds with a spoon. Cut the flesh into small dice and add them to the pineapple.

3 Slit the chili pepper along its length, discard the seeds, and chop it finely.

4 Wash the cilantro or parsley under cold running water, shake dry and finely chop the leaves.

5 Cut the lemon in half and squeeze out the juice, then mix the juice with the finely chopped chili pepper and the chopped cilantro leaves.

6 Season the dressing with salt to taste, then stir the dressing into the fruit. Serve the salad at once.

Tomato Salad

Quick • Central Mexico

Ensalada de jitomate con chilies

Serves 4

1 lb. 5 oz. beefsteak tomatoes
2 fresh medium-hot chili peppers (see Glossary)
small bunch fresh cilantro or flat-leaved parsley (about 1 oz.)
1 lime
3 tbsp. olive oil
salt
freshly ground black pepper
1 garlic clove

Preparation time: 20 minutes

95 cal. per portion

1 Plunge the tomatoes into boiling water. Skin them, cut in half crosswise, and remove the seeds, then coarsely dice the flesh and place it in a bowl.

2 Slit the chili peppers along their length and remove the seeds. Rinse the inside of each chili pepper, then cut them into narrow strips.

3 Wash the cilantro under cold running water and shake dry. Coarsely chop the leaves, then stir them into the tomatoes with the chili peppers.

4 Cut the lime in half and squeeze out the juice, then mix the juice with the olive oil. Season with salt and pepper.

5 Peel and crush the garlic, and stir it into the dressing. Pour the dressing over the salad and serve at once.

Note: This unusual mixture of cool tomatoes and strips of hot, spicy chili peppers would make an exotic first course for a summer or winter menu. Alternatively, it could be served with meat or fish dishes.

Variation: Seed and finely chop a medium-sized cucumber, then mix it into the salad with the chili peppers and the chopped cilantro leaves.

Prickly Pear Leaf Salad

Quick • Central Mexico

Ensalada de nopalitos

Serves 4

4 medium-sized tomatoes (about 1 lb. 5 oz.)
1 Spanish onion
1 jar (about 1 ½ cups) pickled shredded prickly pear leaves (nopalitos en escabeche)
small bunch fresh cilantro or flat-leaved parsley (about ½ oz.)
2 limes

Preparation time: 15 minutes

29 cal. per portion

1 Wash the tomatoes and cut out the hard flesh under the stalks. Cut the tomatoes crosswise into thin slices.

2 Peel the Spanish onion, slice thinly, and separate the slices into rings.

3 Remove the prickly pear leaves and the juice from the jar. On a serving plate or dish, arrange the shredded prickly pear leaves and their juice, the onion rings and sliced tomatoes, side by side in broad stripes (to represent the colors of the Mexican flag).

4 Wash the cilantro, shake it dry, then tear off the leaves and use to garnish the vegetables.

5 Cut the limes into wedges and serve with the salad, so that everyone can season their portion of salad to taste.

Note: The fleshy oval leaves (*nopales*) of the prickly pear cactus are very popular in Mexico, where they are used in a variety of dishes. Pickled prickly pear leaves are available from specialty food stores.

Squid and Bean Salad

Takes time • Jalisco

Ensalada de calamares

Serves 4

2 medium-sized onions
1 bay leaf • 1 tsp. black peppercorns
1 small bunch parsley (about 1 oz.)
• salt
1 lb. 5 oz. squid pouches
1 large green bell pepper
1 fresh medium-hot chili pepper (see Glossary)
1 cup canned kidney beans, drained
juice of 2 lemons
3 tbsp. olive oil
chili powder
freshly ground black pepper

Preparation time: 50 minutes

290 cal. per portion

1 Peel the onions. Cut 1 onion into quarters and place it in a saucepan with the bay leaf, peppercorns, 2 parsley sprigs, and ½ tsp. salt. Add 2 cups water and bring to a boil.

2 Wash the squid, cut them into thin rings, and place in the hot broth in the saucepan. Cover and simmer gently for 20 to 25 minutes, or until tender.

3 Meanwhile, plunge the tomato into boiling water and remove the skin. Cut the tomato in half crosswise, remove the seeds, and finely dice the flesh. Trim and wash the bell pepper, remove the seeds and ribs, and cut the pepper into narrow strips.

4 Slit the chili pepper along its length and remove the seeds. Rinse, then finely chop the flesh.

5 Drain the beans through a sieve, rinse briefly under cold running water, and drain thoroughly. Finely chop the other onion and the rest of the parsley.

6 To make the salad dressing, mix the lemon juice, olive oil, and a little chili powder. Season with salt and pepper.

7 Mix the vegetables and parsley in a bowl. Remove the squid from the broth, drain thoroughly, and allow to cool a little. Add the squid and dressing to the vegetables, toss thoroughly, then serve.

Fish Salad

Straightforward • Veracruz

Ensalada de pescado

Serves 4

1 lb. 5 oz. fresh halibut, cleaned and ready to cook
4 tbsp. olive oil
salt
freshly ground white pepper
2 large beefsteak tomatoes
½ cup olives stuffed with pimientos
3 green onions (scallions)
2 tbsp. capers
2 garlic cloves
3 limes
8 large lettuce leaves for garnish

Preparation time: 30 minutes (plus 2 hours chilling time)

290cal. per portion

1 Preheat the oven to 450 degrees. Rinse the halibut under cold running water and pat dry. Brush a baking dish with 1 tbsp. of the olive oil. Season the fish with salt and pepper, lay it in the prepared dish, and brush it with another 1 tbsp. olive oil.

2 Cover the dish with aluminum foil or a lid and bake the fish in the center of the oven for about 10 minutes. Remove from the oven, leave to cool, then chill in the refrigerator for 2 hours.

3 Plunge the tomatoes into boiling water and remove the skins. Cut in half crosswise, remove the seeds, and dice the flesh. Place the diced tomatoes in a bowl. Finely slice the olives and add the slices to the tomatoes. Trim and wash the green onions (scallions) and cut them into thin rings. Add them to the bowl with the capers. Peel and crush the garlic and stir it into the salad.

4 Squeeze the limes, then mix the juice with the remaining olive oil and season with salt and pepper. Pour the dressing over the salad and toss thoroughly.

5 Wash and dry the lettuce leaves and use them to line four individual plates. Remove the skin and bones from the fish and divide into pieces. Arrange the fish on the lettuce leaves and top with the vegetable mixture.

Limes

Limes are the most cold-sensitive of all the citrus fruits, and for this reason they grow mainly in tropical and subtropical climates, such as southern Mexico. Limes are smaller and juicier than lemons, and have a thin, bright green peel that has a slightly spicy flavor; unlike many lemons, they are not sprayed. The flesh, usually seedless, is a delicate green color and is more aromatic than lemon. While it contains the same minerals as lemon, the vitamin C content of the limes is only one half that of lemons.

Limes are an essential ingredient in Mexican cuisine and are used in the same way as lemons. They can be substituted for lemons in nearly all recipes, but bear in mind you should use slightly less as their flavor is much stronger. Since limes are small and such a pretty color, they make an attractive decoration for long drinks and are popular as a garnish. Limes are now available in supermarkets all year round. When buying them, choose those that feel heavy for their size – it means they are juicy – with bright, clear skin.

BLANCO
LAFIA®
Baja California
HECHO EN MEXICO
Domecq
LOS REYES, EDO. DE MEXICO.
R.F.C. IVP 870122

Mexican Scrambled Eggs

Quick and easy • All regions

Huevos a la mexicana

Serves 4

2 medium-sized beefsteak tomatoes
1 medium-sized onion
2 tbsp. olive oil (see Glossary)
8 eggs
salt • freshly ground black pepper

Preparation time: 25 minutes

230 cal. per portion

1 Plunge the tomatoes into boiling water, remove the skins and seeds, and chop the flesh into small dice. Peel and finely chop the onion.

2 Heat the olive oil in a large skillet and fry the chopped onion over low heat until transparent.

3 Meanwhile, slit the fresh chili pepper along its length, remove the seeds, then wash it, and chop finely. Add it to the onion in the pan.

4 Break the eggs into a bowl. Beat them and season with salt and pepper. Stir in the chopped tomatoes. Pour the egg mixture over the onion in the pan and cook the eggs over medium heat for about 4 minutes until they set, stirring from time to time with a wooden spoon.

Variation: Ranch-style eggs
(*Huevos rancheros*)
Peel and chop 1 onion and 3 garlic cloves, and fry them in 1 tbsp. oil until soft. Add 1 ¼ cups skinned, seeded, and finely chopped tomatoes and 1 finely chopped chili pepper and sauté for about 5 minutes. Prepare 1 cornmeal tortilla (see page 26) and 2 fried eggs per person. Spread the tomato sauce over the tortillas, and top each with 2 fried eggs.

Sausages in Corn Husks

Takes time • Michoacàn

Salchichas en hojas de maíz

Serves 4 (about 15 sausages)

4 dried corn husks (see Note, page 34)
3 cups ground pork or ground mixed meats
1 onion
4 slices white bread
2 eggs
chili powder
4 tbsp. red wine vinegar
3 garlic cloves
1 tsp. dried oregano
1 ½ tsp. salt
chopped fresh cilantro or flat-leaved parsley for garnish

Preparation time: 1 ½ hours (plus 2 to 3 hours soaking time)

550cal. per portion

1 Soak the corn husks in warm water for about 3 hours, then place them in a colander and squeeze out as much moisture as possible. Cut one or two husks lengthwise into strips about ½ inch wide (you need about 15).

2 Place the ground meat in a bowl. Peel and finely chop the onion. Finely crumble the bread in a food processor. Add the onion and bread crumbs to the meat, followed by the eggs, a little chili powder, and the vinegar. Peel and crush the garlic and add to the meat mixture. Season with the cumin, oregano, and salt, and stir thoroughly.

3 Spread out the corn husks. For each husk, shape 2 tbsp. meat filling into a cylinder 3 to 4 inches long. Place it on the corn husk about ¾ inch away from the long edge, leaving plenty of space at either end of the husk.

4 Roll the corn husk over the meat and tie each end with a strip of husk.

5 Place the wrapped packages in batches of four or five in a steamer over a wide saucepan filled with just enough water to reach the base of the steamer. Bring the water to a boil and steam each batch of sausages, covered, for about 15 minutes. Keep the cooked sausages warm in a low oven while cooking the rest.

6 Arrange the sausages on a serving platter. Open the corn husks and sprinkle with chopped cilantro.

Note: Mexican Salsa (see page 54) or Devil Sauce (see page 57) are very good accompaniments to serve with this dish.

Stuffed Squash Blossom

More complex • All regions

Flor de calabaza rellena

Serves 4

12 zucchini squash with blossoms (see Note)
¾ cup cream cheese
4 tbsp. freshly grated queso añejo (see Glossary), or Parmesan
2 tbsp. Green Tomato Sauce (see page 58)
1 to 2 tbsp. all-purpose flour
2 eggs
salt
freshly ground black pepper
2 cups vegetable oil

Preparation time: 45 minutes (plus 35 minutes for making the Green Tomato Sauce)

260 cal. per portion

1 Carefully dip the squash blossoms in a bowl of cold water, then leave them to drain on paper towels.

2 Place the cream cheese in a bowl and stir in the *queso añego* and the Green Tomato Sauce, and mix well.

3 Fill the squash blossoms with equal quantities of the cheese mixture, then carefully press the tips of the flowers over the filling (*above*).

4 Sprinkle the flour into a shallow bowl. Whisk the eggs in a second bowl and season with salt and pepper.

5 Heat the oil in a wide saucepan, then briefly coat the squash blossoms in the flour and dip them in the egg. Fry the blossoms in the hot oil over high heat for 2 to 3 minutes until golden-brown. Remove them from the saucepan with a slotted spoon. Drain on paper towels.

Variation: Peel and finely chop 1 small onion and sauté in 1 tbsp. oil. Trim, wash, and finely chop 1 cup mushrooms and add them to the onion. Peel and crush 1 garlic clove, add it to the pan, and sauté until most of the liquid evaporates. Season with salt, pepper, and a little chili powder. Stir in 2 tbsp. grated Parmesan cheese and use the mixture to fill eight prepared squash blossoms. Arrange the squash blossoms in a steamer. Fill a saucepan with water to a level of about 1 inch and bring to a boil, then steam the squash blossoms for about 15 minutes.

Note: Squash blossoms, a common sight in markets throughout Mexico, are available from May through September in Mexican food stores throughout the Southwest and in other cities with Mexican populations. They are served as a vegetable with onions, garlic, and chili peppers, and in soup; single blossoms also make a very attractive garnish. Squash blossoms should be used as quickly as possible after picking, as they soon wither.

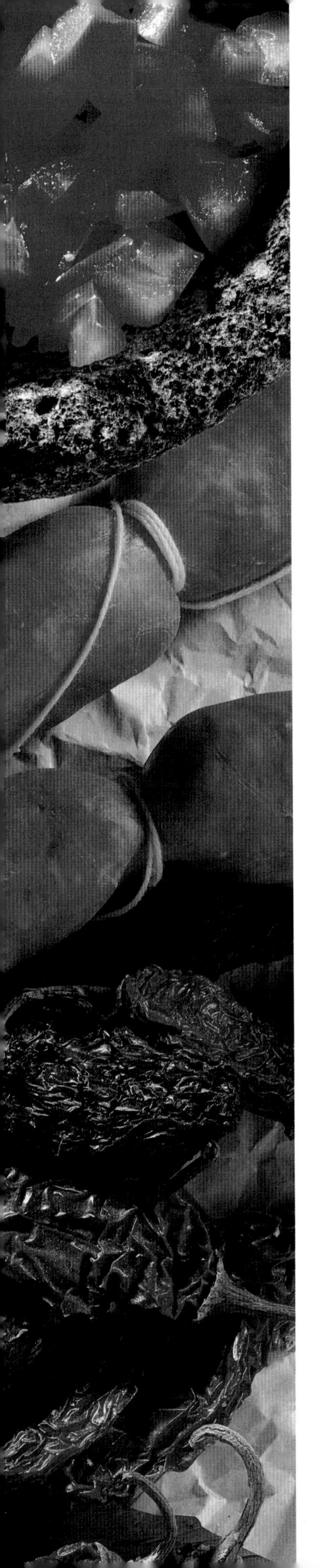

SAUCES, SOUPS, AND STEWS

The delicious cold sauces known as salsas are an important ingredient of practically any Mexican dish, including tortillas, meat, poultry, and fish. Salsas are based on chopped onions, red or green tomatoes, lots of chili peppers, and chopped cilantro. One exception is guacamole, a subtly spiced avocado dip.

The most famous of the Mexican hot sauces is the luxurious mole, which consists of dried chili peppers, various spices, and ground nuts. In Mexico, and in specialty food stores, you can buy ready-made moles in powdered or paste form. Recipes for these sauces are given in the meat and poultry chapter on page 89, since they are not merely side dishes but an intrinsic part of the entrée.

When it comes to soup, Mexicans distinguish between *sopa seca*, dry soup, and *sopa aguada*, liquid soup. After a selection of little snacks, such as potato chips, olives, and varieties of tortilla, the real meal begins with a *sopa aguada*; this may be a clear broth with pieces of chicken and sliced avocado, a creamy corn or mushroom soup, or a refreshing, chilled avocado soup. A *sopa seca* usually consists of rice, and is served as an in-between course. Recipes for these soups can be found in the rice chapter on page 73. The Mexicans also cook substantial, hearty concoctions of lentils or beans, with slices of chorizo sausage or meat, that are more akin to stews than soups.

Cooked Chili Sauce

Salsa frita

Spicy • All regions

Serves 6

3 cups beefsteak tomatoes
2 fresh or canned jalapeño peppers (see Glossary)
1 small onion • 1 garlic clove
2 tbsp. vegetable oil
small bunch fresh cilantro (about ½ oz.)
salt • freshly ground black pepper

Preparation time: 30 minutes (plus 30 minutes cooling time)

50 cal. per portion

1 Plunge the tomatoes into boiling water, remove the skins and seeds, and finely chop the flesh. Wash the chili peppers if using fresh, then remove the seeds, and finely chop the chilies.

2 Peel and finely chop the onion. Peel and crush the garlic. Heat the oil in a sauté pan and fry the onion until soft, then add the garlic. Stir in the tomatoes and chili peppers. Cover and simmer over low heat for about 15 minutes.

3 Meanwhile, wash the cilantro and shake dry. Tear the leaves from the stalks and chop them finely. Season the sauce with salt and pepper, and leave to cool. Serve the sauce cold, sprinkled with the finely chopped cilantro.

Note: Choose hot chili peppers, such as jalapeño, for an authentic strong, spicy flavor. If you prefer a milder flavor, use a milder type of chili pepper.

Red Bean Sauce

Salsa de frijoles rojos

Quick sauce • All regions

Serves 6

1 cup canned kidney beans
1 small onion • 2 garlic cloves
salt • freshly ground black pepper
chili powder

Preparation time: 20 minutes

160cal. per portion

1 Drain the kidney beans through a sieve, reserving the liquid. Purée the beans with half the liquid in a blender or food processor.

2 Peel the onion and finely chop it. Peel and crush the garlic. Heat the oil in a saucepan and fry the onion until transparent. Add the crushed garlic and fry briefly.

3 Add the puréed beans and cook over low heat for about 5 minutes, stirring frequently. The sauce should have a creamy texture.

4 Season generously with salt, pepper, and chili powder. Serve the sauce hot.

Mexican Salsa

Salsa mexicana

Speedy sauce • All regions

Serves 6

1½ cups tomatoes • 2 large onions
2 fresh chili peppers (see Glossary)
juice of 1 lime
small bunch cilantro (about 1 oz.)
salt • freshly ground black pepper

Preparation time: 20 minutes

26 cal. per portion

1 Plunge the tomatoes into boiling water, remove the skins and seeds, and finely dice the flesh. Place the chopped tomatoes in a bowl.

2 Peel and finely chop the onions, then stir them into the bowl. Slit the chili peppers lengthwise, remove the seeds, then wash and finely chop the flesh. Add it to the bowl with the tomatoes. Stir in the lime juice.

3 Wash and chop the cilantro, and stir it into the sauce. Season with salt and pepper, then chill the sauce in the refrigerator until ready to serve it.

MEXICO

Avocado Dip

Guacamole

Quick and easy • All regions

Serves 4 to 6

2 medium-sized beefsteak tomatoes
1 small onion
3 fresh or canned jalapeño peppers (see Glossary)
4 ripe avocados
2 limes
small bunch fresh cilantro or flat-leaved parsley (about 1 oz.)
salt
freshly ground black pepper

Preparation time: 30 minutes

330 cal. per portion

1 Plunge the tomatoes into boiling water, then remove the skins, and finely chop the flesh. Peel and very finely. Chop the onion.

2 Slit one chili pepper along its length, remove the seeds, wash if using fresh, and chop the flesh as finely as possible.

3 Peel the avocados, cut them in half lengthwise, and pit them. Scrape off any flesh still attached to the shell. Cut the limes in half and squeeze out the juice. Purée the avocados and lime juice in a blender.

4 Mix the puréed avocados, tomatoes, onion, and chopped chili pepper. Wash the cilantro or parsley, shake dry, and finely chop the leaves. Stir them into the avocado mixture and season with salt and pepper.

5 Before serving, cut the remaining chili peppers in half crosswise, then slit them lengthwise and remove the seeds. Arrange the chili pepper slices on top of the dip.

Note: Serve the dip with small, crisply fried pieces of tortilla, or tortilla chips.

For a tasty starter or light vegetarian lunch, serve crisply cooked cauliflower topped with guacamole.

Devil Sauce

Salsa endiablada

Very hot • Oaxaca

Serves 4

3 dried ancho chili peppers (see Glossary)
½ small onion
1 garlic clove

Preparation time: 45 minutes

4 cal. per portion

1 Preheat the oven to 300 degrees. Lay the chili peppers on a cookie sheet and roast in the center of the oven for about 5 minutes to bring out the flavor. Remove them from the oven and leave to cool.

2 Slit the chili peppers along their length and carefully remove the seeds and stalks. Place the chili peppers in a small saucepan with ¾ cup cold water.

3 Peel and coarsely chop the onion and garlic. Add to the chili peppers in the pan, cover, and simmer over low heat for about 30 minutes, until the chili peppers are soft enough to be able to purée them.

4 Transfer the contents of the pan to a food processor or blender and process to at thick, reddish-brown purée. Serve the sauce cold.

Note: This sauce can be kept in the refrigerator for about two weeks. It goes will with tortillas, enchiladas, and many other dishes.

Green Tomato Sauce

Quick and easy • All regions

Tomatillo salsa

Serves 4 to 6

1 ¼ cups canned tomatillos (see below)
1 fresh or canned jalapeño pepper (see Glossary)
½ cup chicken broth
1 garlic clove
small bunch cilantro or flat-leaved parsley (about 1 oz.)
juice of 1 lime
salt
lime slices and cilantro leaves for garnish (optional)

Preparation time: 20 minutes (plus 15 minutes cooling time)

11 cal. per portion (if serving 6)

1 Strain the canned tomatillos through a sieve and leave to drain thoroughly.

2 Wash the chili pepper if using fresh, and deseed. Place the tomatillos, chili pepper, and broth in a saucepan.

3 Peel and crush the garlic and add it to the tomatillos and jalapeño in the saucepan. Simmer, uncovered, over low heat for about 5 minutes, stirring the mixture frequently.

4 Purée the cooked mixture in a food processor or blender. Rub the purée though a fine sieve and leave to cool.

5 Wash the cilantro and shake dry, then tear off the leaves and chop them finely. Stir the lime juice and cilantro into the sauce and season with salt. Serve the sauce cold, garnished with lime slices and cilantro, if liked.

Variation: To add extra body to the sauce, coarsely mash the flesh of 1 ripe avocado in a bowl and stir in the juice of 1 lime. Add 1 finely chopped onion and then stir the mixture into the green tomato sauce.

Tomatillos

Native to Mexico, and also known as Mexican green tomatoes, *tomates verdes, tomates de cáscara*, or *fresadillas*, these fruits do indeed resemble green tomatoes in a thin, parchment-like husk. They are, in fact, a variety of physalis, from the same family as the Peruivan ground cherry or Cape gooseberry.

Tomatillos turn yellow when fully ripe, but are usually used green and unripe. Cooking them brings out their full flavor – a blend of tomato and lemon – but they have an interesting sharpness when raw. In Mexican cuisine, they are mainly used in sauces. Small, unripe tomatoes can be used instead, but the taste is not the same.

To prepare fresh tomatillos, strip off the papery husks and rinse the fruit under cold running water. Place them in a saucepan, cover with water, and simmer over low heat until tender.

Fresh tomatillos are not widely available outside Mexican neighborhoods. Canned tomatillos can be obtained from specialty food stores. Fresh tomatillos can be stored in the refrigerator for two to three weeks, wrapped in paper.

Spicy Bean Stew

Time consuming • Jalisco

Frijoles sazonados estilo jalisco

Serves 4 to 6

2 cups dried pinto or borlotti beans
4 tbsp. lard
2 medium-sized onions
8 garlic cloves
7 oz. chorizos (see Glossary)
1 fresh red, medium-hot chili pepper for garnish (see Glossary)
salt
freshly ground black pepper

Preparation time: 30 minutes (plus 12 hours soaking time and 2 hours cooking time)

520 cal. per portion (if serving 6)

1 Soak the beans overnight in cold water. The next day, drain off the water and put the beans in a large saucepan.

2 Add 2 ½ quarts fresh water. Reserve 1 tbsp. lard and add the rest to the pan with the beans. Peel and slice 1 onion and add to the beans.

3 Bring to a boil and boil vigorously for 10 minutes, then partly cover the pan with the lid and cook over medium heat for about 1 ½ hours, or until the beans are tender.

4 Drain the beans, reserving the cooking water. Peel and finely chop the second onion and the garlic. Heat the reserved 1 tbsp. lard in a saucepan and fry the onion and garlic until soft.

5 Meanwhile, skin the chorizos and cut into slices ¼ inch thick. Add the beans and sausages to the saucepan. Add about 1 cup of the bean cooking water and simmer, uncovered, over medium heat for about 10 minutes, or until the broth begins to thicken.

6 Meanwhile, wash the chili pepper and cut it in half crosswise. Scrape out the seeds with a knife and slice it into thin rings.

7 Season the spicy beans with salt and pepper to taste, and serve sprinkled with the chili rings.

Chorizo Soup

Sopa de chorizo con nopales

Sustaining • Central Mexico

Serves 4

2 cups canned prickly pear leaves (nopales al natural)
14 oz. chorizos (see Glossary)
1 medium-sized onion
½ green bell pepper
1 fresh or canned jalapeño pepper (see Glossary)
1 quart chicken broth
small bunch cilantro or flat-leaved parsley (about 1 oz.)
2 medium-sized tomatoes
½ cup sour cream

Preparation time: 45 minutes

710 cal. per portion

1 Place the prickly pear leaves in a colander and rinse under cold running water, then drain thoroughly.

2 Skin the chorizos and cut into slices about ½ inch thick. Peel and finely chop the onion. Trim, wash and dice the bell pepper. Wash the chili pepper if using fresh, deseed and chop finely.

3 Fry the sliced chorizos in a saucepan or fireproof casserole, without fat, over low heat, until lightly browned.

4 Pour off the fat from the sausages. Add the onion, bell pepper, and chili pepper and stir-fry over low heat for about 5 minutes, until softened.

5 Add the chicken broth and the prickly pear leaves to the soup, bring to a boil, cover, and simmer over low heat for 15 to 20 minutes.

6 While the soup is cooking, prepare three side dishes which correspond to the Mexican national colors of green, white, and red.

7 Wash the cilantro or parsley, shake dry and finely chop the leaves, then place them in a bowl. Wash the tomatoes, remove the seeds, and finely chop the flesh. Place the tomatoes in a separate bowl. Pour the sour cream into third bowl. Serve these side dishes with the soup, so everyone can help themselves.

Veracruz-style Soup

Sopa veracruzana

Easy • Gulf of Mexico

Serves 4

1 lb. 5 oz. red snapper or ocean perch fillets
juice of 1 lemon • salt
freshly ground black pepper
1 small onion • 2 garlic cloves
7 oz. carrots
7 oz. floury potatoes
3 tbsp. olive oil
2 cups tomatoes
3 tsp. capers
10 green olives, pitted
4 tbsp. rice • 2 eggs
small bunch cilantro or flat-leaved parsley (about 1 oz.)

Preparation time: 1 hour

400 cal. per portion

1 Rinse the fish fillet under cold running water, pat dry, and cut into 1-inch pieces. Sprinkle with lemon juice, season with salt and pepper, cover and leave to stand in the refrigerator.

2 Meanwhile, peel the onion and garlic. Finely chop the onion. Peel the carrots and slice thinly. Peel the potatoes, wash them and cut into ½ inch dice.

3 Heat the olive oil in a wide saucepan and sauté the chopped onion over low heat. Crush the garlic and add it to the onion. Add the carrots and potatoes, and sauté for about 5 minutes.

4 Meanwhile, plunge the tomatoes into boiling water, remove the skins, and coarsely chop the flesh. Add it to the other ingredients in the pan. Add the capers and the olives, and 1 quart water. Season with salt and pepper, and bring to a boil. Add the rice, cover, and simmer for about 25 minutes.

5 Hard-boil the eggs for 10 minutes, then shell and finely chop them. Wash the parsley, shake dry, then tear off the leaves and chop finely.

6 Taste the soup and season with salt and pepper, if necessary. Stir in half the chopped egg and half the parsley. Add the fish pieces, cover, and simmer for 5 minutes, until the fish is cooked.

7 Serve the fish soup in warmed soup plates, sprinkled with the other half of the chopped egg and parsley.

Chicken and Avocado Soup

Caldo de pollo con aguacates

Easy • All regions

Serves 4

1 small onion
1 quart chicken broth
4 chicken breast fillets (about 7 oz. each)
1 fresh medium-hot chili pepper (see Glossary)
1 ripe avocado • juice of ½ lemon
small bunch cilantro or flat-leaved parsley (about 1 oz.)
salt • freshly ground black pepper

Preparation time: 40 minutes

330 cal. per portion

1 Peel and finely chop the onion. Bring the chicken broth to a boil in a large saucepan. Add the chicken breast fillets and onion, cover, and simmer over low heat for about 20 minutes.

2 Slit the chili pepper along its length, remove the seeds, then rinse and slice it thinly.

3 Peel the avocado, then cut it in half lengthwise and pit it. Cut the flesh lengthwise into long, narrow wedges and sprinkle them immediately with the lemon juice.

4 Remove the chicken breasts from the broth, cut them crosswise into narrow strips, and keep warm. Meanwhile, cook the sliced chili pepper in the hot broth for about 5 minutes.

5 Wash the cilantro, shake dry, then tear off the leaves and chop them fairly coarsely. Arrange the chicken strips, avocado wedges, and cilantro in four soup bowls. Season the hot chicken broth with salt and pepper, and pour it into the soup bowls. Serve at once.

Mushroom Soup

Sopa de hongos

Easy • Central Mexico

Serves 4 to 6

1 medium-sized onion
4 cups button mushrooms
2 tbsp. olive oil
2 ¾ cups beefsteak tomatoes
2 fresh or canned jalapeño peppers (see Glossary)
3 cups beef broth (made with a bouillon cube)
salt
freshly ground black pepper
small bunch fresh cilantro or flat-leaved parsley (about 1 oz.)

Preparation time: 45 minutes

69 cal. per portion (if serving 6)

1 Peel and finely chop the onion. Trim the mushrooms and rinse briefly under cold running water, then slice thinly. Heat the oil in a saucepan and sauté the onion over low heat until soft.

2 Add the mushrooms and continue to cook the vegetables over low heat for about 10 minutes.

3 Meanwhile, plunge the tomatoes into boiling water, remove the skins, and finely chop the flesh. Wash the chili peppers if using fresh, then deseed and finely chop. Add to the other vegetables in the saucepan with the tomatoes.

4 Pour the broth over the vegetables, season to taste with salt and pepper, then cover and simmer over medium heat for about 15 minutes.

5 Wash the cilantro, shake dry, tear off the leaves, chop them coarsely, and sprinkle into the soup before serving.

Note: If you are short of time, use canned tomatoes with their juice instead of the fresh tomatoes.

Variation: Use oyster mushrooms instead of the button mushrooms or try a mixture of both types.

Potato Soup with Egg

Sopa de papa y huevo duro

Easy • Guerrero

Serves 4

1 ¼ cups floury potatoes
2 eggs
1 small onion
1 tbsp. vegetable oil
2 garlic cloves
3 cups beef broth
salt
freshly ground black pepper
1 large beefsteak tomato
small bunch fresh cilantro or flat-leaved parsley (about 1 oz.)

Preparation time: 55 minutes

140 cal. per portion

1 Wash the potatoes, but do not peel them, then place in a saucepan with just enough water to cover them. Cover the pan and cook over medium heat for 20 to 30 minutes.

2 Meanwhile, hard-boil the eggs for about 10 minutes. Rinse them in cold water and leave to cool.

3 Peel and finely chop the onion. Heat the oil in a saucepan and sauté the onion over low heat. Peel and crush the garlic and add to the onion.

4 Peel the potatoes and mash until smooth. Add the mashed potatoes to the onions in the pan. Pour in the beef broth and season with salt and pepper, then cover and simmer the soup over low heat for about 10 minutes.

5 Plunge the tomato into boiling water, then remove the skin and cut the flesh into small dice. Stir the diced tomato into the pan.

6 Shell and finely chop the hard-boiled eggs. Wash the cilantro or parsley, shake dry, finely chop the leaves, and stir half of them into the soup.

7 Season the soup to taste and pour it into four soup bowls. Serve sprinkled with the chopped hard-boiled egg and the remaining cilantro leaves.

Lentil Soup with Pineapple

Takes time • Oaxaca

Sopa de lentejas

Serves 4 to 6

1 cup lentils
4 slices bacon
1 tbsp. vegetable oil
1 medium-sized onion
4 cups beef broth
8 oz. floury potatoes
salt
freshly ground black pepper
chili powder
1 small or ½ large pineapple
juice of 1 lime

Preparation time: 35 minutes (plus 12 hours soaking time and 45 minutes cooking time)

290 cal. per portion (if serving 6)

1 Place the lentils in a large bowl and cover with cold water. Leave them to soak overnight.

2 The next day, discard the rind from the bacon slices, then cut them into small pieces. Heat the oil in a saucepan and fry the bacon over low heat until the fat runs.

3 Meanwhile, peel and finely chop the onion, add it to the bacon, and sauté briefly. Drain the lentils in a sieve, then add to the pan with the broth. Bring the mixture to a boil, cover, and simmer over low heat for about 45 minutes, until the lentils are almost tender (see Note, right).

4 Peel and wash the potatoes. Cut them into small dice and stir into the lentils. Season generously with salt, pepper, and chili powder. Return briefly to a boil, then simmer, covered, over low heat for about 15 minutes.

5 While the soup is cooking, peel the pineapple and chop the flesh into small dice. Stir the diced pineapple into the soup with the lime juice and briefly heat through. Taste the soup and adjust the seasoning, if necessary.

Note: The cooking time for lentils depends on how fresh they are. It is not always easy to tell with pulses, and the only way is to keep testing them for tenderness as they cook. Adjust the cooking time accordingly.

Cream of Sweetcorn Soup

Easy • Colima

Crema de elote

Serves 4

1 medium-sized onion
1 tbsp. olive oil
3 cans sweetcorn (about 2¾ cups)
3 cups chicken broth
salt
freshly ground black pepper
juice of ½ lime
small bunch of cilantro or flat-leaved parsley (about 1 oz.)

Preparation time: 40 minutes

260 cal. per portion

1 Peel and finely chop the onion. Heat the olive oil in a saucepan and sauté the chopped onion.

2 Drain the sweetcorn thoroughly in a sieve. Add two thirds of the sweetcorn to the pan. Add the broth, bring to a boil, cover, and simmer over low heat for about 20 minutes.

3 Purée the soup in a food processor or blender, then pass it through a fine sieve. Return the soup to the pan. Add the rest of the sweetcorn.

4 Bring the soup briefly to a boil and stir in the lime juice. Season to taste with salt and pepper.

5 Rinse the cilantro, shake dry, and coarsely chop the leaves. Stir them into the soup, and serve at once.

Variation: You can substitute fresh corn, instead of canned, when it is in season.

Black Bean Soup

Takes time • Jalisco

Sopa de frijol negro

Serves 4

1 cup dried black beans
1 bay leaf
2 fatty bacon slices
3 tbsp. vegetable oil
1 large onion
1 beefsteak tomato
1 quart beef broth
1 tsp. dried oregano
salt • freshly ground black pepper
3 sprigs epazote or lemon balm (see opposite)
2 cornmeal tortillas (see page 26), made the day before
4 tsp. sour cream

To garnish:
4 slices of lime or lemon
a few leaves of fresh cilantro or flat-leaved parsley

Preparation time: 1 ½ hours (plus 12 hours soaking time)

430 cal. per portion

1 Place the beans in a bowl and cover with cold water. Leave them to soak overnight. The next day, drain them and transfer to a saucepan. Cover with cold water and add the bay leaf. Bring to a boil and boil vigorously for 10 minutes, then cover and cook over medium heat for about 40 minutes, or until they are tender. Drain through a sieve; discard the bay leaf. Grind the beans to a fine purée in a food processor or blender.

2 Chop the bacon into small dice. Heat 1 tbsp. oil in a saucepan and brown the bacon. Peel and finely chop the onion, add to the bacon and fry over medium heat until transparent. Peel and crush the garlic and add to the pan.

3 Plunge the tomato into boiling water, remove the skin and seeds, and finely chop the flesh. Add the chopped tomato and bean purée to the ingredients in the pan. Add the broth and the oregano, and season with salt and pepper. Cover the pan and simmer over low heat for about 15 minutes.

4 Wash the epazote or lemon balm and shake dry. Tear off the leaves, cut them into strips, and stir into the soup. To make totopos, cut the tortillas into narrow strips and fry them in the rest of the oil over high heat until crisp.

5 Check the seasoning, then pour the soup into four soup cups or plates. Add a teaspoonful of sour cream to each one. Sprinkle with the totopos. Garnish each portion with a slice of lime or lemon and one or two cilantro leaves.

Wine: a Mexican *vin ordinaire* goes will with this black bean soup.

Epazote and Cilantro

Epazote and cilantro are the two most important herbs in Mexican cooking. Epazote, which has a lemony taste and is used fresh, is an essential ingredient in Mexican bean dishes. It is also used for making herbal tea. If you can bring some epazote seeds from Mexico, the herb can easily be grown in a flower pot. It also grows wild in some parts of the United States. Lemon balm, used fresh and dried, is a good substitute.

The delicate leaves of cilantro, also known as fresh coriander or Chinese parsley, have an intensely aromatic flavor that goes will with meat, poultry, and fish dishes, as well as vegetables. They are particularly good with chili peppers, much used in Mexican cuisine.

Fresh cilantro is widely available. Alternatively, you can easily cultivate it yourself from seed. If you cannot obtain cilantro, parsley can be substituted, but the taste is not the same. Cilantro does not dry well and is always used fresh. It is very sensitive to heat, so for the best results its should only be added to cooked dishes right at the end of the cooking time.

Chick-pea Stew

Time consuming • All regions

Caldo de indianilla

Serves 4

1 cup dried chick-peas (garbanzo beans)
4 garlic cloves
4 oz. carrots
½ cup rice
4 chicken thigh joints (about 7 oz. each)
2 fresh medium-hot chili peppers (see Glossary)
juice of 1 lime
salt • freshly ground black pepper
1 oz. fresh cilantro
1 oz. flat-leaved parsley
1 small onion

Preparation time: 1½ hours (plus 12 hours soaking time)

500 cal. per portion

1 Place the chick-peas in a bowl and cover with cold water. Leave to soak overnight.

2 The next day, drain off the water. Peel the garlic and place 1 clove in the pan with the chick-peas. Cover with a scant 1 litre water. Bring to a boil and boil vigorously for 10 minutes, then cover and cook over medium heat for a further 5 minutes.

3 Meanwhile, peel and thinly slice the carrots. Add the carrots and the rice to the pan and stir. Lay the chicken joints on top and continue to cook, covered, for about 30 minutes, until the chicken joints and chick-peas are tender.

4 Remove the chicken joints, skin them and detach the meat from the bones. Cut the meat into 1 inch pieces.

5 Deseed and wash the chili peppers, and chop them finely. Add the chopped chili peppers to the pan with the chicken pieces. Crush the rest of the garlic and add to the other ingredients. Stir in the lime juice and season with salt and pepper. Wash the cilantro and parsley, shake dry and finely chop the leaves. Stir them into the stew.

6 Peel and finely chop the onion and sprinkle it over the stew before serving.

Chilled Avocado Soup

Quick and easy • Yucatán

Sopa fría de aguacates y cilantro

Serves 4

2 ripe avocados
2 limes
1 large cucumber
1 small onion
small bunch of fresh cilantro or flat-leaved parsley (about 1 oz.)
2 cups chicken broth
salt
freshly ground white pepper
3 slices white bread
2 tbsp. butter
2 garlic cloves • sweet paprika
chili powder

Preparation time: 30 minutes (plus 2 hours chilling time)

380 cal. per portion

1 Peel, halve, and pit the avocados. Coarsely chop the flesh and place it in a food processor or blender. Squeeze the limes and pour the juice over the chopped avocados.

2 Peel the cucumber and cut it in half lengthwise. Scrape out the seeds with a spoon. Chop the cucumber halves into large chunks and add them to the food processor or blender.

3 Peel the onion, cut it into quarters, and add to the other ingredients. Blend the avocado mixture to a purée, then rub it through a fine sieve into a bowl.

4 Wash the cilantro, shake dry, and finely chop the leaves. Stir them into the purée with the chicken broth and season well with salt and pepper.

5 Cover the bowl and chill the soup in the refrigerator for about 2 hours.

6 Meanwhile, cut the sliced bread into small dice. Heat the butter in a skillet and fry the diced bread until crisp and golden-brown.

7 Peel and crush the garlic and spread it over the bread. Season the croûtons with salt, pepper, and a little paprika and chili powder, and leave to cool.

8 Stir the soup thoroughly, then pour it into four soup bowls. Serve at once, sprinkled with the croutons.

VEGETABLES, RICE, AND BEANS

A Mexican vegetable market is a veritable feast for the senses. On market days, farmers and peasants from all over the surrounding countryside descend on the towns and villages with their freshly picked fruits and vegetables. These brightly colored wares, artistically arranged in baskets or bowls, are stacked high on stalls or just spread out on the ground.

Many of the vegetables on display, such as zucchini, Swiss chard, avocados, and spinach, are familiar to all Americans and are easy to obtain here. Others, such as the *camote*, a nutty flavored sweet potato, or *chayote*, (*mirliton*) a yellowish-green pear-shaped squash, are more familiar in the southwestern United States and the Mexican neighborhoods of other cities.

In Mexico, vegetables are often served as a meal in themselves, or as a separate course, rather than as a side dish. The same applies to rice, which is prepared in a variety of interesting ways – with pomegranate seeds and banana (see page 83), for example. Rice dishes, in the form of a *sopa seca* or "dry soup," are often served before the fish or meat entrée.

Dried beans play a very important role in Mexican cuisine. Even before the Spaniards arrived they were a staple food, and they are still eaten nearly every day, served either as a side dish, or in soups and stews, as the basis for sauces, or as a purée.

Zucchini and Sweetcorn

Calabacitas con elote

Easy • Oaxaca

Serves 4

14 oz. small zucchini
1 medium-sized red bell pepper
1 can sweetcorn (about 1 ⅓ cups) or 3 to 5 fresh ears of corn
1 medium-sized onion
¼ cup butter
2 garlic cloves
salt
freshly ground black pepper

Preparation time: 30 minutes

170 cal. per portion

1 Wash and top-and-tail the zucchini and slice them thinly. Wash the bell pepper, then cut it into quarters and remove the seeds and ribs. Cut the pepper quarters first into strips and then into small dice.

2 If you are using canned sweetcorn, drain it thoroughly through a sieve. If using fresh corn, remove and cook the corn kernels (see Note).

3 Peel and finely chop the onion. Heat the butter in a wide, sauté pan, and fry the onion over medium heat until transparent. Add the zucchini, bell pepper, and sweetcorn.

4 Peel and crush the garlic and add to the pan. Stir thoroughly, season with salt and pepper, then cover and sauté the vegetables over medium heat for about 10 minutes.

Note: If you are using fresh corn, you must first detach the corn kernels from each cob with a sharp knife. Cook the corn in boiling salted water for about 3 minutes and drain thoroughly. Add the corn to the onion with the zucchini and bell pepper, as above.

This dish can be served as a separate course or as a side dish with meat.

Fried Chayote

Chayote con jitomate

Simple • Central Mexico

Serves 4

1 medium-sized chayote (see Glossary) or 1 lb. 5 oz. zucchini
1 large beefsteak tomato
1 large onion
2 garlic cloves
1 to 2 fresh or canned jalapeño peppers (see Glossary)
2 tbsp. vegetable oil
salt
small bunch of cilantro or flat-leaved parsley (about 1 oz.)

Preparation time: 45 minutes

86 cal. per portion

1 Discard the stalk of the chayote and cut it first into slices, then into ½ inch dice. If using zucchini, top-and-tail them, and cut into ½ inch dice.

2 Plunge the tomato into boiling water, remove the skin, and finely chop. Peel the onion and the garlic, and finely chop. Wash the chilies if using fresh.

3 Heat the oil in a skillet and sauté the onion, garlic, and whole chilies over low heat until tender. Stir in the tomato and ¾ cup water and cook for 3 minutes. Stir in the diced chayote or zucchini and season with salt, cover and cook for about 10 minutes.

4 Meanwhile, wash the cilantro, shake dry, and finely chop the leaves. Taste the vegetables and add extra salt and pepper, if necessary. Sprinkle the chopped cilantro over the top and serve at once.

Note: This spicy dish can be served as a vegetarian main course or as an accompaniment to meat, poultry and fish. It is also very good sprinkled with a little Cheddar or Parmesan cheese.

Sweet Potatoes with Tequila

Camotes con limas y tequila

Serves 4 to 6

Fall dish • Central Mexico

2 ¼ lb. sweet potatoes or small waxy potatoes
½ cup butter
2 tsp. sugar
1 tbsp. lime juice
1 tbsp. tequila
salt
freshly ground black pepper
2 limes

Preparation time: 45 minutes

290 cal. per portion (if serving 6)

1 Peel the sweet potatoes, and then cut them into halves or quarters, according to their size. Cut the pieces into slices ½ inch thick.

2 Heat the butter in one very large skillet or two smaller ones over medium heat; do not allow it to brown. Add the sliced sweet potatoes to the pan and sprinkle the sugar on top.

3 Fry the potatoes over medium heat for 15 to 20 minutes, stirring from time to time, until the slices are transparent and lightly caramelized.

4 Stir the lime juice and tequila into the potatoes and cook for a further 2 to 3 minutes. Season to taste with salt and pepper.

5 Wash the limes and cut them into long, thin wedges. Serve the potatoes accompanied by the lime wedges, so that everyone can add more lime juice according to taste.

Note: Sweet potatoes may be served as a separate course. They also make a delicious accompaniment to pork and poultry dishes.

Tequila

Tequila, Mexico's most famous spirit – and its favorite drink – is named for a little town not far from Guadalajara, in Jalisco. It is made from the fermented sap of cactus-like plants belonging to the agave family. This clear, fiery spirit has been brewed in Mexico ever since the Spaniards introduced the process of distillation.

Mescal, also distilled from agave plant juice – its name derives from metl, the Indian for agave – is similar to tequila, but stronger. It is made in the Oaxaca region and is famous for the dead worm that is put into each bottle. Tequila goes through two distillation processes to achieve the desired purity. After the second stage, the spirit is crystal clear and is sold as "fino." Alternatively, it can then be aged in oak casks, which gives it a delicate golden-yellow color and a subtle flavor.

Traditionally served in a glass rimmed with salt, accompanied by wedges of lime or lemon, tequila is also used to make cocktails such as the cointreau-laced Margarita, and Tequila Sunrise, a taller drink made with orange juice and grenadine.

HECHO EN MEXICO
700 ml.
NOM-1102-I

Stuffed Peppers

Easy • Guerrero

Chiles rellenos

Serves 4

8 small green bell peppers or large green sweet peppers (about 3 ½ oz. each) or 8 canned poblano chilies (see Glossary)
3 tbsp. cream cheese
1 egg
4 fresh medium-hot chili peppers (see Glossary)
small bunch of cilantro or flat-leaved parsley (about 1 oz.)
salt
freshly ground black pepper
1 onion
2 garlic cloves
1 tbsp. olive oil
1 bay leaf

Preparation time: 55 minutes

170 cal. per portion

1 Wash the bell peppers, cut off the tops, and remove the seeds and cores (*above*). If using poblano chilies, prepare them in the same way.

2 Stir the cream cheese and the egg together in a bowl. Slit 2 of the medium-hot chili peppers lengthwise and remove the seeds. Wash them, and chop finely. Wash the cilantro, shake dry and finely chop the leaves. Stir the chopped chili peppers and cilantro into the cheese mixture, and season with salt and pepper.

3 Using a teaspoon, carefully fill the prepared peppers with the cheese mixture (*above*).

4 Peel and finely chop the onion. Heat the oil in a wide saucepan or fireproof casserole and fry the onion over low heat until transparent. Peel and crush the garlic and add it to the onion.

5 Plunge the tomatoes into boiling water, remove the skins and coarsely chop the flesh. Add the tomato to the pan with the bay leaf, and season with salt and pepper. Cover and simmer over medium heat for about 5 minutes.

6 Place the bell peppers, filled side upward, on top of the tomato sauce and continue to cook, covered, over low heat for about 20 minutes. Meanwhile, cut the remaining chili peppers in half crosswise through the middle, scrape out the seeds with a knife, and cut the chili peppers into the rings.

7 Serve two stuffed peppers per person on warmed individual plates with the tomato sauce, garnished with the chili pepper rings. If the peppers were cooked in a flameproof casserole, garnish and serve them straight from the dish, if preferred.

Variation: Instead of cream cheese, make the filling for the bell peppers with 1 ¾ cups ground meat, 1 egg, 1 small onion, 2 small garlic cloves, and 1 small chili pepper, chopped and sautéed, and 1 tbsp. fresh bread crumbs. Cook as described above.

Refried Beans

Frijoles refritos

Traditional speciality • Guerrero

Serves 4 to 6

2 cups dried black or pinto beans
1 medium-sized onion
⅓ cup lard or melted, lightly browned butter
1 tsp. salt

To garnish (optional):
feta cheese, tortilla chips, tomato wedges, and sliced cucumber

Preparation time: 30 minutes (plus 12 hours soaking time and 2 ½ hours cooking time)

520 cal. per portion (if serving 6)

1 Place the beans in a bowl and cover with water. Leave to soak overnight.

2 The next day, drain the beans, then transfer them to a saucepan. Cover with fresh water to a level about 1 inch above the beans. Peel the onion, chop into chunks, and add to the beans.

3 Bring to a boil and boil vigorously for 10 minutes, then partly cover the pan with its lid and simmer over low heat for 2 to 2½ hours, until the beans are very soft and easy to mash. Stir the beans frequently during the cooking time, and add a little more hot water if they begin to dry out.

4 Place the beans in a food processor or blender with the lard and salt, and process to a thick purée.

5 Transfer the bean purée to a large skillet and stir-fry, without fat, for about 10 minutes, until the purée is firm and dry.

6 Spoon 2 to 3 tbsp. of the beans onto four to six individual plates or bowls. Sprinkle with crumbled feta cheese and garnish with tortilla chips, tomato wedges, and sliced cucumber, if liked. Serve with devil sauce (see page 57).

Variation: Spread refried beans on crisply toasted tortillas, topped with chicken, onion rings, sliced tomato, and avocado.

Beans

Beans are one of Mexico's most important staple foods, and no meal is considered complete without a dish of some sort of *frijoles*, or dried beans (as distinct from green beans, known as *ejotes*.) Beans are a valuable source of essential vitamins and minerals, and are also high in protein. Together with corn (see page 84), they have formed the basis of a simple but balanced diet in Mexico since precolonial times.

Throughout Mexico, beans are available in an amazing range of different sizes and colors – black, white, red, brown, mottled purple, speckled, and even bright yellow. They appear on the menu in soups and stews, as vegetables, puréed or as a sauce ingredient, and are served at any meal from breakfast to late dinner.

Before cooking, dried beans should always be soaked, preferably overnight, in plenty of cold water. The next day, immerse them in fresh water without salt, in a large saucepan, and boil briskly for about 10 minutes to eliminate any toxins. Then reduce the heat and simmer, stirring from time to time, until tender. The overall cooking time will depend on how long the dried beans have been stored, so it is best to test them frequently during cooking and adjust the length of time accordingly. Never salt beans until they are cooked, salt toughens the skins.

Mexican Rice

Arroz a la mexicana

Easy • All regions

Serves 4

1 ¾ cups beefsteak tomatoes
1 onion
1 garlic clove
1 cup beef broth
¾ cup long-grain rice
salt
freshly ground black pepper
⅓ cup thawed frozen peas and very finely diced carrots for garnish (optional)

Preparation time: 40 minutes

200 cal. per portion

1 Plunge the beefsteak tomatoes into boiling water, remove the skins, and coarsely chop the flesh.

2 Peel and coarsely chop the onion and garlic, then purée the onion and garlic with the tomatoes in a food processor or blender. Transfer the purée to a saucepan, add the beef broth, and bring to a boil.

3 Stir in the rice, cover, and simmer over low heat for about 25 minutes, until the rice is tender. Season with salt and pepper and serve at once, garnished with the frozen peas and diced carrots, if using.

Variation: Green rice
(Arroz verde)
Finely chop 1 small onion and 2 garlic cloves, and sauté them in 1 tbsp. oil. Prepare 2 cups leaf spinach and add to the pan. Add 4 tbsp. cilantro leaves to the vegetables. Sauté for about 5 minutes, season with salt and pepper, then purée in a food processor or blender. Return the purée to the pan and stir in 1 cup cooked rice and 1 or 2 finely chopped fresh green chili peppers.

Note: This dish is a typical sopa seca, or "dry soup," often served before a fish, meat, or poultry course.

Rice with Pomegranate

Arroz con granadas

Easy • Chiapas

Serves 4

1 ¼ cups beefsteak tomatoes
scant 2 cups chicken broth
1 medium-sized onion
3 tbsp. vegetable oil
2 garlic cloves
⅔ cup long-grain rice
salt
freshly ground black pepper
1 pomegranate
1 banana
juice of ½ lemon
1 sprig cilantro or flat-leaved parsley

Preparation time: 40 minutes

260 cal. per portion

1 Plunge the tomatoes into boiling water, remove the skins, and finely chop the flesh. Bring the chicken broth to a boil in a saucepan, add the tomatoes, return to a boil, and simmer over low heat for a few minutes.

2 Meanwhile, peel and coarsely chop the onion. Heat the oil in a saucepan and fry the onion over low heat until transparent. Peel and crush the garlic and add to the onion. Sprinkle the rice into the pan and stir until all the grains are coated with a film of oil.

3 Pour in the hot broth and tomato mixture, season with salt and pepper, then cover and simmer over low heat for 20 to 25 minutes.

4 While the rice is cooking, cut the pomegranate in half and scoop out the seeds. Peel and slice the banana and sprinkle with lemon juice. Rinse the cilantro under cold running water, shake dry, and tear off the leaves.

5 Stir the pomegranate seeds and two-thirds of the sliced banana into the cooked rice. Serve at once, garnished with the remaining banana slices and the cilantro leaves.

Variation: Rice with sweetcorn
(Arroz con elote)
Instead of adding pomegranate seeds and banana, stir 1 small can drained sweetcorn and 1 chopped, fresh medium-hot chili pepper into the rice.

Sweetcorn Gratin

Easy • Central Mexico

Budín de elote

Serves 4 to 6

1 large onion
1 large red bell pepper
1 large green bell pepper
2 tbsp. olive oil plus extra for greasing the baking dish
3 garlic cloves
2 cans sweetcorn (about 2 ⅓ cups each)
4 eggs
3 tbsp. all-purpose flour
1 tsp. sugar
salt
freshly ground black pepper
chili powder

Preparation time: 1 hour

430 cal. per portion (if serving 6)

1 Preheat the oven to 400 degrees.

2 Peel and finely chop the onion. Trim and wash the red and green bell peppers, and cut them first into strips, then into small dice.

3 Heat the oil in a wide skillet and sauté the chopped onion and peppers. Peel and crush the garlic, add to the pan, and continue to sauté the mixture for about 5 minutes.

4 Drain the canned sweetcorn through a sieve and grind it in a food processor or blender. Whisk the eggs in a large bowl. Add the sweetcorn purée, the pepper-and-onion mixture, and the flour. Stir thoroughly and then season with the sugar and little salt, pepper, and chili powder.

5 Grease a suitable baking dish, pour in the mixture, and bake in the center of the oven for 30 to 40 minutes, or until the top is golden.

Note: This sweetcorn gratin is a tasty and unusual accompaniment to serve with meat dishes. Alternatively, served on its own it makes a good vegetarian lunch or dinner.

Corn

Corn was once the generic name for any of the cereal grains. In U.S. English, it has become synonymous with maize, which after wheat, is the world's most important staple food. There are many different colors of corn, often known as Indian corn in the U.S., including black, white, yellow, and red, though not all of them are easy to find outside the southwestern United States.

Mexico's warm climate is perfect for the cultivation of corn, and it has been grown here for some 7,000 years. The Aztecs regarded it as a sacred plant, as did the Mayas. Along with dried beans, it is one of the mainstays of the Mexican diet. Corn is also ground to make cornmeal. *Masa harina*, a specially processed fine cornmeal, is used in Mexico for making the tortillas that accompany almost every meal. It can be bought in Mexican stores. Cornstarch, is a finely ground white starch extracted from corn kernels. Because it is so fine, it makes a very good thickening agent, particularly for sauces. Unlike wheat flour, it contains no gluten.

Beans in Beer

Takes time • Colima

Frijoles borrachos

Serves 4

1 cup dried pinto or kidney beans
1 cup beefsteak tomatoes
1 large onion
4 slices fat bacon
1 tbsp. vegetable oil
3 garlic cloves
2 fresh or canned jalapeño peppers (see Glossary)
1 tsp. chopped fresh oregano
1 tsp. ground cumin
salt
freshly ground black pepper
2 cups beer

Preparation time: 30 minutes (plus 12 hours soaking time and 1 ½ hours cooking time)

430 cal. per portion

1 Place the beans in a bowl and cover with water. Leave to soak overnight.

2 Plunge the tomatoes into boiling water, remove the skins, and coarsely chop the flesh. Peel and finely chop the onion. Remove the bacon rind and cut the slices into thin strips.

3 Heat the oil in a flameproof casserole or saucepan and briefly fry the bacon. Add the onion. Crush the garlic and add to the pan. Sauté for about 3 minutes over medium heat. Stir in the tomatoes.

4 Wash the chili peppers. If using fresh ones, deseed and chop them finely.

5 Drain the beans and put them in a saucepan with enough cold water to cover. Bring to a boil and boil vigorously for 10 minutes, then drain and add to the casserole with the chili peppers. Add the oregano and cumin, and season with salt and pepper.

6 Add the beer, bring slowly to a boil, then cover and simmer over low heat for 1 to 1 ½ hours, or until the beans are tender.

Green Beans with Limes

Easy • Guanajuato

Ejotes con limón

Serves 4

1 lb. 5 oz. young green beans
salt
small bunch of flat-leaved parsley (about 1 oz.)
5 tbsp. butter
2 limes
a little sugar
freshly ground black pepper
lime slices for garnish (optional)

Preparation time: 25 minutes

130 cal. per portion

1 Wash the green beans and trim them. Bring plenty of salted water to a boil and cook the beans for about 7 minutes, until they are tender but still crisp.

2 Meanwhile, wash the parsley, shake dry, and finely chop the leaves.

3 Melt the butter in a small saucepan over low heat. Squeeze the limes and add the juice and parsley to the butter. Season with a little sugar, salt, and pepper.

4 Drain the beans in a colander, then transfer them to a bowl and stir in the butter and lime dressing, mixing well. Garnish with slices of lime, if liked, and serve at once.

Note: The beans can be served as a separate course or as a side dish with fish, meat, or poultry.

MEAT AND POULTRY

The earliest Indian tribes of Mexico lived mainly on corn, beans, chili peppers, avocados, pumpkins, and fish. It was a well-balanced but not very varied diet. Meat was seldom eaten, and then only by the wealthier sectors of the population, who enjoyed such rich fare as wild rabbit, venison, and turkey. Along with a particular breed of duck, turkey was the only poultry kept by the Mayas.

Things changed dramatically with the arrival of the Spanish conquistadors in the early 16th century. The Spaniards introduced chickens, sheep, goats, pigs, and cattle, and continued to breed them. As a result, the native diet was enriched not only with new kinds of meat, but also with other related animal products such as cheese, milk, eggs, and animal fats.

Pork is still very popular today, and is prepared Spanish style. For example, cooked pork crackling is sprinkled with lime juice and salt to make the crispy cocktail snack *chicharrón*. Both chorizo, spicy paprika sausage, and *longaniza*, another type of sausage, are made as they are in Spain. In northern Mexico, where high-grade cattle are reared on the region's rich, sweeping pastures, people generally prefer beef, often in the form of large juicy steaks.

Chicken, another favorite, is served in every region, usually with different sauces. It is also a very popular filling for tortillas, tacos, enchiladas, and tamales. Turkey is mainly reserved for important occasions, and is served either marinated (*en escabeche*), or with a traditional rich *mole* sauce.

Yucatán-style Leg of Lamb

Takes time • Southern specialty

Pierna de cordero estito yucateco

Serves 4 to 6

1 tsp. ground achiote (see Glossary, and Note, page 105)
salt
½ tsp. freshly ground black pepper
3 tbsp. olive oil
1 boned leg of lamb (you may have to order this from your butcher in advance), about 2 ½ lb.
1 onion
½ cup fresh bread crumbs
1 tbsp. grated rind of an untreated orange
3 to 5 tbsp. orange juice
1 tsp. grated rind of an untreated lemon
½ cup sour cream
small bunch of cilantro or flat-leaved parsley (about 1 oz.)
½ cup beef broth

Preparation time: 1 hour (plus 2 hours cooking time)

570 cal. per portion (if serving 6)

1 Mix the achiote with salt, pepper, and 2 tbsp. olive oil and rub the leg of lamb with the mixture. Preheat the oven to 400 degrees.

2 Peel and finely chop the onion, then place it in a mixing bowl with the fresh bread crumbs. Stir in the grated orange rind, orange juice, grated lemon rind, and the sour cream.

3 Wash the cilantro, shake dry, finely chop the leaves, and stir them into the other stuffing ingredients. Spread the stuffing on the inside of the leg of lamb (*above*).

4 Roll the meat, starting at the narrow edge, and tie it with kitchen string.

5 Heat the rest of the oil in a roasting pan and sear the meat over high heat until well browned all over. Pour the beef broth over the meat (*above*), cover with a lid or foil, and cook in the center of the oven for 2 hours, removing the lid or foil after 1 hour.

6 Remove the meat from the oven, cover to keep warm, and leave to stand for about 15 minutes. Discard the string and cut the meat into thin slices. Serve with Sweet Potatoes with Tequila (see page 76) and Green Beans with Limes (see page 87).

Note: In the Jalisco and Michoacán regions of western Mexico, mutton and goat are prepared in the same way as this lamb recipe.

Pork Chops with Beans

Easy • Quintana Roo

Chuletas de cerdo con frijoles

Serves 4

1 large onion
1 green bell pepper
3 tbsp. olive oil
2 garlic cloves
1 cup canned kidney beans
½ cup beef broth
salt • freshly ground black pepper
few drops of tabasco sauce
4 pork chops (about 7 oz. each)
4 tbsp. shredded Jack or Cheddar cheese

Preparation time: 40 minutes

670 cal. per portion

1 Peel and finely chop the onion. Trim, wash, and finely dice the bell pepper. Heat 1 tbsp. oil in a skillet and fry the chopped onion and pepper over low heat until the onion is translucent. Crush the garlic and add it to the pan.

2 Strain the kidney beans through a sieve, rinse briefly under cold running water, and drain thoroughly.

3 Add the beans to the pan, then stir in the broth . Season with salt and pepper and Tabasco sauce. Cover and simmer over low heat for about 15 minutes.

4 Meanwhile, rinse the pork chops in cold running water, pat dry, and season with pepper on both sides. Heat the remaining 2 tbsp. oil in a skillet and fry the chops over high heat for about 10 minutes, turning once. Season with salt when they are cooked.

5 Arrange the chops on four warmed plates, spoon the bean mixture around them, and serve with the shredded cheese sprinkled on top.

Note: Serve with cornmeal or wheat tortillas (see page 26 and 28).

Pork with Fruit

Takes time • Oaxaca

Mancha manteles

Serves 4 to 6

5 dried ancho chili peppers (see Glossary)
2¼ lb. pork fillet
4 tbsp. vegetable oil
1 small onion
4 garlic cloves
10 blanched almonds
1-inch piece cinnamon stick
½ tsp. each of cloves, dried oregano, and thyme
½ tsp. crushed peppercorns
2 cups ripe beefsteak tomatoes
1 tsp. salt • ¼ tsp. sugar
4 very firm bananas
4 slices fresh pineapple
2 tbsp. butter

Preparation time: 35 minutes

(plus 45 minutes cooking time)
450 cal. per portion

1 Slit the ancho chilies along their length and remove the seeds and ribs. Stir-fry the chilies in a dry skillet for about 5 minutes, then soak them in hot water for about 20 minutes.

2 Cut the pork into slices about the thickness of a finger. Heat the oil in a saucepan or a flameproof casserole and sear the pork over high heat. Remove the meat from the pan and keep warm.

3 Peel the onion and garlic and cut into chunks. Stir-fry them in the meat fat with the almonds, cinnamon stick, cloves, oregano, thyme, and crushed peppercorns for about 5 minutes.

4 Plunge the tomatoes into boiling water, skin, and chop finely. Add to the spices in the pan and fry briefly. Drain the chili peppers and add them to the other ingredients in the pan. Transfer the contents of the pan to a blender or food processor and purée to a thick, reddish-brown sauce.

5 Return the sauce to the pan. Add the salt, sugar and a scant cup of water and simmer, uncovered, over low heat for about 10 minutes, stirring from time to time. Lay the meat in the sauce, cover, and cook over medium heat for a further 20 minutes.

6 Peel the bananas. Cut the bananas and pineapple slices into small pieces. Heat the butter in a skillet and fry the fruit until golden-brown. Reserve a few well-shaped pieces to use as a garnish. Add the rest of the fruit to the meat and simmer over low heat for a further 5 to 10 minutes. Garnish with the reserved fruit and serve with rice.

Ragout of Pork with Capers

Straightforward • Southern Mexico

Cerdo con alcaparras

Serves 4

1 large onion
2 tbsp. lard
3 garlic cloves
⅓ cup ground almonds
3 cloves
1-½-inch piece cinnamon stick
1 tsp. peppercorns
1 ¾ cups beefsteak tomatoes
1 lb. 10 oz. pork spare ribs
2 tbsp. capers, drained
⅓ cup pitted green olives
3 pickled or canned chili peppers
1 ¾ cups beef broth

Preparation time: 1 ½ hours

760 cal. per portion

1 Peel and coarsely chop the onion. Heat 1 tbsp. lard in a skillet and brown the onion. Peel and crush the garlic and add it to the pan.

2 Add the almonds, cloves, cinnamon stick, and peppercorns, and fry over low heat for about 10 minutes, stirring frequently. Discard the cloves and the cinnamon stick.

3 Transfer the rest of the contents of the skillet to a blender or food processor and grind to a purée.

4 Plunge the tomatoes into boiling water, remove the skins and the seeds, then coarsely chop the flesh.

5 Cut the meat into ½-inch dice. Heat the rest of the lard in a wide saucepan or a fireproof casserole and fry the meat in batches over high heat until it is well browned on all sides.

6 Return all the browned meat to the pan. Add the vegetable purée, chopped tomatoes, capers, and olives.

7 Cut the chili peppers into rings and stir them into the meat mixture, then add the beef broth.

8 Cook the pork ragout, covered, over medium heat for about 45 minutes, stirring frequently. If necessary, adjust the seasoning before serving.

Pork Loin with Zucchini

Spicy • Toluca

Lomo de cerdo con calabacitas

Serves 4

2 ¼ cups beefsteak tomatoes
2 medium-sized onions
1 lb. 10 oz. loin of pork
2 tbsp. lard
2 garlic cloves
1 lb. 5 oz. zucchini
salt
freshly ground black pepper
1 tsp. cayenne pepper
3 tbsp. feta cheese

Preparation time: 50 minutes

480 cal. per portion

1 Plunge the tomatoes into boiling water, remove the skins and seeds, and coarsely chop the flesh. Peel and finely chop the onions.

2 Cut the pork loin into ½ inch dice. Heat the lard in a large saucepan or a fireproof casserole and fry the diced meat until well browned on all sides. Remove it from the pan and set aside.

3 Fry the onions in the fat remaining in the pan, until they are transparent. Peel and crush the garlic, add it to the onions, and fry briefly.

4 Stir the chopped tomatoes into the pan and then cook the mixture over low heat for about 5 minutes.

5 Meanwhile, wash and top-and-tail the zucchini. Cut them lengthwise into quarters and then into pieces about the same size as the diced meat.

6 Stir the meat and zucchini into the pan. Season with salt, pepper and the cayenne pepper. Cover and cook over medium heat for about 20 minutes.

7 Meanwhile, coarsely grate the feta cheese. Sprinkle it over the top of the ragout just before serving. Serve with Mexican salsa (see page 54).

Pork Fillet with Peanuts

Easy • Valladolid

Lomo en salsa de cacahuates

Serves 4

1 lb. 12 oz. pork fillet
salt
freshly ground black pepper
cayenne pepper
3 tbsp. vegetable oil
⅓ cup unsalted, shelled peanuts
1 medium-sized onion
1 cup beefsteak tomatoes
12 pitted black olives • 2 cloves
3 to 4 cm piece cinnamon stick
1 ½ cups beef broth
1 ¾ cups small waxy potatoes, unpeeled
4 rindless fat bacon slices
1 tbsp. lard
small bunch fresh cilantro or flat-leaved parsley (about 1 oz.)

Preparation time: 1 hour

860 cal. per portion

1 Remove the skin and fat from the pork fillet, rinse the fillet under cold running water, and pat dry. Season all over with salt and pepper and sprinkle with a little cayenne pepper.

2 Heat the oil in a large saucepan or a fireproof casserole and brown the meat over high heat. Remove it from the pan, cover, and keep warm.

3 Fry the peanuts in the meat fat until they are golden-brown. Meanwhile, peel and finely chop the onion. Plunge the tomatoes into boiling water, remove the skins and seeds, then coarsely chop the flesh, and add it to the peanuts. Stir in the chopped onion.

4 Coarsely chop the olives and add to the pan with the cloves and cinnamon stick. Season with salt and pepper. Add the broth and simmer, uncovered, over low heat for about 10 minutes.

5 Lay the meat in the sauce, cover the pan and cook over medium heat for about 25 minutes. Meanwhile, cook the unpeeled potatoes for 10 minutes, or until tender, then peel them.

6 Chop the bacon into small dice. Heat the lard in a large skillet and fry the bacon until the fat runs. Toss the potatoes in the fat.

7 Wash the cilantro or parsley, shake dry, then finely chop the leaves and sprinkle them over the potatoes and bacon.

8 Remove the meat from the sauce and carve across the grain into thick slices. Season the sauce with salt and pepper and serve with the meat and potatoes.

Fillet Steak Mexican Style

Spicy • Chihuahua

Puntas de filete a la mexicana

Serves 4

1 lb. 5 oz. fillet steak
1 medium-sized onion
1 garlic clove
2 cups beefsteak tomatoes
4 fresh medium-hot chili peppers (see Glossary)
2 tbsp. vegetable oil • 1 tsp. vinegar
salt • freshly ground black pepper
small bunch cilantro or flat-leaved parsley (about 1 oz.)

Preparation time: 1 hour

240 cal. per portion

1 Slice the meat then cut in into narrow strips. Peel the onion and garlic. Finely chop the onion. Plunge the tomatoes into boiling water, remove the skins and seeds, and coarsely chop the flesh.

2 Slit each of the chili peppers along its length, remove the seeds, wash the peppers, and cut into narrow strips.

3 Heat the oil in a wide skillet and sear the strips of meat, in batches, over high heat. Remove the meat from the pan and reduce the heat.

4 Fry the onion in the fat remaining in the pan until transparent. Stir in the tomatoes and chili peppers.

5 Crush the garlic and add to the pan. Season with the vinegar, and salt and pepper. Cover the pan and simmer over medium heat for about 10 minutes.

6 Add the strips of meat and the juices to the sauce and heat through for about 5 minutes. Wash the cilantro or parsley, shake dry and finely chop, then stir it into the meat. Serve with boiled rice.

Chili Rabbit

Conejo enchilado

Takes time • Northern Mexico

Serves 4 to 6

1 rabbit (about 4 lb. 8 oz., ask your butcher to cut it into serving pieces) or 4 lb. 8 oz. rabbit joints
salt
freshly ground black pepper
3 oz. dried pasilla or ancho chili peppers (see Glossary)
10 garlic cloves
1 large beefsteak tomato
small bunch flat-leaved parsley (about 1 oz.)
4 tbsp. vegetable oil
1 tbsp. white wine vinegar
1 tsp. caraway seeds

Preparation time: 1½ hours (plus 30 minutes marinating time)

570 cal. per portion (if serving 6)

1 Briefly rinse the rabbit joints under cold running water and pat dry. Season all over with salt and pepper, and place the joints in a bowl.

2 To make the marinade, slit the chili peppers along their length and remove the seeds. Peel the garlic. Plunge the beefsteak tomato into boiling water, remove the skin, then cut the flesh into eight wedges. Wash the parsley, shake dry, and tear off the leaves.

3 Heat 2 tbsp. oil in a large skillet and stir-fry the chili peppers and garlic cloves over medium heat for 5 minutes. Add the tomato, half the parsley leaves, the vinegar, and caraway seeds. Season with salt and pepper, and heat through.

4 Transfer the contents of the pan to a food processor or blender and process to a thick purée.

5 Coat the rabbit pieces with the spicy purée. Cover and leave to marinate in the refrigerator for about 30 minutes.

6 Heat the rest of the oil in a flameproof casserole and add the rabbit and chili purée. Stir in most of the remaining parsley and 1 cup water.

7 Cover the casserole and cook over low heat or bake in the center of the oven at 375 degrees for about 45 minutes, or until the rabbit is tender. Serve at once, sprinkled with the rest of the parsley.

Note: Chicken or turkey portions can be prepared in the same way.

Chicken with Walnut Sauce

Pechugas en nogada

Straightforward • Central Mexico

Serves 4

1 cup chicken broth
4 chicken breast fillets (about 7 oz. each)
8 oz. red bell peppers
⅓ cup walnut meats
⅓ cup sour cream
⅓ cup cream cheese
salt
freshly ground black pepper

Preparation time: 45 minutes

550 cal. per portion

1 Preheat the oven to 450 degrees. Bring the broth to a boil in a saucepan. Place the chicken breast fillets in the broth, cover the pan, and simmer over medium heat for about 25 minutes. Remove from the broth and keep warm. Reserve the broth.

2 Meanwhile, trim and wash the bell peppers and cut in half lengthwise. Place on a wire rack and bake in the center of the oven for about 20 minutes, until the skins are brown and blistered.

3 Meanwhile, finely grind the walnuts in a food processor. Transfer them to a saucepan and stir in the sour cream, cream cheese, and ¾ cup of the reserved chicken broth. Simmer the sauce for about 5 minutes, then season to taste with salt and pepper.

4 Peel the peppers and cut into narrow strips. Arrange the chicken on a warm serving dish and pour the walnut sauce over the top. Serve garnished with the strips of red bell pepper.

Turkey Mole

Mole poblano de guajolote

Takes time • Pueblo
Serves 8 to 10

4 tbsp. lard
1 turkey (about 9 lb.s), cut into serving portions
salt
2 large onions • 13 garlic cloves
6 dried guajillo chili peppers (see Glossary)
4 dried ancho chili peppers
3 dried pasilla chili peppers
3 tbsp. vegetable oil
4 cups beefsteak tomatoes
⅓ cup blanched almonds
4 tbsp. shelled peanuts
4 tbsp. sesame seeds
4 cm piece cinnamon stick
½ tsp. aniseed
⅓ cup raisins
ground cloves • ground coriander
3 ½ oz. unsweetened chocolate
freshly ground black pepper
lime and tomato wedges for garnish

Preparation time: 2 hours

980 cal. per portion (if serving 10)

1 Preheat the oven to 425 degrees. Heat the lard in a roasting pan and brown the turkey portions on all sides, then season with salt. Peel and chop the onions and garlic cloves. Add half the onion and about one quarter of the chopped garlic to the turkey. Add about 2 quarts water. Cover and cook in the center of the oven for 1 ½ hours.

2 Slit the chili peppers along their length and remove the seeds and ribs. Heat the oil in a skillet and fry the chili peppers for 2 minutes. Transfer them to a bowl, cover with hot water, and leave to soak for about 25 minutes. Plunge the tomatoes into boiling water and remove the skins and seeds. Purée the flesh in a food processor or blender and pour it into a saucepan.

3 Fry the almonds and peanuts in the fat in which the chilies were cooked over medium heat, until golden-brown, then transfer to a bowl. Fry 2 tbsp. of the sesame seeds, the cinnamon stick, and aniseed in the same fat, and add to the bowl. Fry the remaining onion and garlic. Season with the ground cloves and coriander. Pour the contents of the skillet and the bowl into the food processor or blender. Drain the chili peppers and add them, then purée.

4 Add the purée to the tomato purée and simmer for 5 minutes. Crumble the chocolate and stir it into the sauce. Remove turkey from the pan. Measure 3 cups broth and add them to the sauce, then simmer over medium heat for about 15 minutes, stirring frequently.

5 Lay the turkey in the sauce, season with pepper, and simmer over low heat for 10 to 15 minutes. Toast remaining sesame seeds in a dry skillet, sprinkle them over the dish, garnish and serve.

Cocoa and Chocolate

When the Spaniards were received as guests at the royal Aztec court, they were introduced to a drink made from powdered cocoa beans. Its name, *xocolatl* – derived from two Aztec words, *xococ* meaning bitter and *atl* meaning water – is the origin of the word chocolate.

The cocoa tree is native to Mexico. Its large pods, which are hacked from the branches when ripe, contain 20 to 30 white seeds, or beans, embedded in a white pulp. These beans are heaped up, covered, and left to ferment. After five to ten days, during which time the tannin oxidizes, the pulp dissolves, and the beans turn dark brown, the characteristic cocoa flavor develops. The beans are then dried, roasted, and ground, and the fat extracted. The resulting smooth brown cocoa mass is processed into cocoa powder, cocoa butter, or chocolate.

Today, Mexicans make a sweet chocolate from ground cocoa beans mixed with cinnamon, ground almonds, and sugar which is pressed into round, flat discs. When dissolved in hot milk or water, it makes a delicious drink. Chocolate is also one of the principal ingredients in the famous Mexican *mole poblano* sauce.

Chicken with Pineapple

Not difficult • Oaxaca

Pollo con piña

Serves 4

1 oven-ready chicken (about 2 lb. 12 oz.)
1 onion
2 garlic cloves
1 red bell pepper
1 green bell pepper
1 medium-sized pineapple
2 tbsp. vegetable oil
salt • freshly ground black pepper
2 cloves • 1 bay leaf
1-2 inch piece cinnamon stick
1 sprig fresh thyme
1 cup chicken broth

Preparation time: 45 minutes (plus 30 minutes cooking time)

550 cal. per portion

1 Rinse the chicken under cold running water, pat it dry, and divide into six to eight serving pieces. Peel and finely chop the onion and place it in a bowl. Peel and crush the garlic and add to the onion.

2 Cut the bell peppers into quarters, trim, wash, and chop into small dice. Remove the crown of leaves from the pineapple. Peel the pineapple, cut into quarters, and discard the hard core. Chop the flesh into small pieces and mix with the diced peppers.

3 Preheat the oven to 400 degrees. Heat the oil in a skillet and fry the chicken joints over medium heat until golden-brown on all sides. Season with salt and pepper and remove from the pan.

4 Fry the onion and garlic in the remaining fat until transparent. Add the pepper and pineapple mixture and season with salt and pepper. Add the cloves, bay leaf, cinnamon stick, and thyme. Pour in the chicken broth.

5 Arrange the chicken pieces on top of the vegetables and bake, uncovered, in the center of the oven for about 30 minutes. Serve with rice.

Chicken Mole

Takes time • La Garita

Pollo en mole verde

Serves 4

1 oven-ready chicken (2 lb. 12 oz. to 3 lb. 5 oz.)
2 onions
salt
½ cup peeled pumpkin seeds (pepitas)
4 tbsp. blanched almonds
4 tbsp. walnut meats
2 garlic cloves
2 tbsp. lard
1 ¼ cups canned tomatillos
1 large can poblano chilies
2 to 3 canned jalapeño chilies
1 fresh red chili pepper for garnish (see Glossary)

Preparation time: 1 hour (plus 1 hour cooking time)

860 cal. per portion

1 Place the chicken in a saucepan or a flameproof casserole and add enough cold water to cover. Peel one onion and cut into chunks. Add the onion chunks to the pan or casserole and season with salt. Bring to a boil, then cover, and cook the chicken over medium heat for about 30 minutes.

2 Remove the chicken from the pan and allow it to cool a little, then divide it into six or eight portions, and remove the skin. Strain the cooking liquid through a sieve and reserve.

3 Stir-fry the pumpkin seeds, almonds, and walnuts in a skillet without fat over medium heat, until the pumpkin seeds burst. Place the nut mixture in a blender and finely grind.

4 Peel and finely chop the remaining onion and the garlic. Heat the lard in a skillet and fry the onion and garlic until transparent. Drain the tomatillos. Drain the poblano and jalapeño peppers, remove the stalks and seeds, and cut the flesh into strips. Add the chili peppers and tomatillos to the onion and sauté over medium heat for about 10 minutes.

5 Stir in the nut mixture and ½ cup of the broth and simmer, covered, over low heat for a further 5 minutes. Pour into a blender and process to a thick purée, then return the purée to the pan and season with salt. Place the chicken in the sauce, cover, and heat through for 10 minutes. Garnish with chopped fresh chili pepper and serve at once.

Marinated Turkey

Pavo en escabeche

Takes time • Campeche

Serves 8 to 10

1 oven-ready turkey (6 lb 8 oz. to 9 lb.), cut into serving pieces (see Note)
3 tbsp. achiote powder (see Note and Glossary)
¾ cup orange juice
1 tbsp. white wine vinegar
2 cups well-seasoned chicken broth
2 ¼ lb. red onions
6 fresh hot chili peppers (see Glossary)
4 garlic cloves
2 tsp. dried oregano
1 tsp. ground cumin
1 tsp. salt

Preparation time: 45 minutes (plus 1 ½ hours cooking time)

760 cal. per portion (if serving 10)

1 Preheat the oven to 400 degrees. Rinse the turkey joints under cold running water and pat dry. Using the tip of a sharp knife, make several incisions 1 to 2 inches deep in the skin side of the joints.

2 Mix the achiote powder, 2 tbsp. of the orange juice, and the vinegar to a thick paste in a bowl.

3 Rub the turkey pieces all over with the paste, spreading it under the skin and into the incisions.

4 Arrange the turkey pieces in a large roasting pan and pour the broth over the meat. Cover and cook in the center of the oven for 1 to 1 ½ hours, or until the meat is tender.

5 Meanwhile, peel and very thinly slice the red onions. Wash the fresh chili peppers, then remove the seeds and cut the flesh into strips.

6 Roast the unpeeled garlic with the oregano and cumin in a skillet without fat, until the cumin starts to give off its aroma.

7 Peel the garlic cloves, then crush them with the oregano and cumin, using a pestle and mortar.

8 Remove the turkey joints from the broth and drain well. Pour the chicken

broth into a bowl, allow to cool a little, then skim off the fat from the top.

9 Preheat the broiler and broil the turkey pieces on a rack placed over the grill pan for about 20 minutes, or until the skin is crisp, turning the pieces from time to time to brown on all sides.

10 Meanwhile, pour 1 cup of the cool chicken broth into a saucepan. Add the garlic mixture, salt, sliced onions, and remaining orange juice. Cover the pan and cook the mixture over medium heat for 10 to 15 minutes, then stir in the strips of hot chili pepper.

11 Arrange the turkey pieces on a large serving dish or individual plates, and cover with the onion and chili mixture. Serve warm or cold.

Note: You may need to order the turkey cut into serving pieces in advance from your butcher.

If you are unable to find achiote powder, you can use the following paste instead. Peel and crush 8 garlic cloves and put in a bowl. In a separate bowl, mix 1 tsp. each of ground cloves, allspice, cumin, and coriander, and 1 to 1 ½ tsp. ground cinnamon. Mix in 1 tsp. coarsely ground pepper, 2 tsp. dried oregano, a little cayenne pepper, and 1 tsp. chili powder. Stir the mixture into the crushed garlic, then stir in 2 tbsp. orange juice and 1 tbsp. white wine vinegar.

FISH AND SEAFOOD

Mexico is blessed with a wealth of fish and seafood. The Pacific, the Gulf of Mexico, the Gulf of California, and the Caribbean all yield a rich selection, which is prepared in endlessly inventive ways by sophisticated restaurants and simple beachside huts alike.

For those who like their fish or seafood unadulterated, it can be simply broiled with a touch of garlic and a sprinkling of lime juice, but there are many other delicious methods that are equally easy to follow at home. One popular dish that is well worth trying is *ceviche*, raw, firm-fleshed fish which is marinated and served ice-cold.

Mexico's commonest fish is the *huachinango*, the red snapper. A favorite way of preparing it is *a la veracruzana*, with tomatoes and a variety of spicy ingredients. Other readily available fish are swordfish, squid, mackerel, and sea bass, as well as many varieties less well-known to Americans. There are all kinds of shellfish, too: shrimp and lobsters, spiny lobsters, oysters, and mussels.

In inland areas, fish and seafood are less readily available, and are more likely to be sold in preserved form, for example, dried shrimp of various sizes and bacalao, the same dried salted cod that is popular in Spain. These can be bought in any Mexican market.

Red Snapper Veracruz Style

Easy • Gulf of Mexico

Huachinango a la veracruzana

Serves 4

1 onion
2 tbsp. olive oil
2 cups beefsteak tomatoes
4 tbsp. green olives, pitted
2 tbsp. capers
3 fresh guero or medium-hot chili peppers (see Glossary)
salt
freshly ground black pepper
2¼ lb. red snapper or ocean perch fillets
juice of 1 lemon

Preparation time: 45 minutes

290 cal. per portion

1 Peel and finely chop the onion. Heat the olive oil in a wide saucepan and fry the onion until soft.

2 Plunge the tomatoes into boiling water, remove the skins and stalks, and purée the flesh in a food processor or blender, then rub through a fine sieve. Cut the olives in half and place them in a saucepan with the capers and tomato purée. Wash the chili peppers, remove the seeds, then cut them into rings, and stir into the tomatoes.

3 Simmer the sauce, uncovered, over medium heat for about 5 minutes, until it begins to thicken. Season generously with salt and pepper.

4 Wash the fish and pat dry. Sprinkle it with lemon juice and season with salt and pepper. Lay the fillets in the sauce, cover, and simmer over low heat for 6 to 8 minutes, until cooked through. Serve with rice.

Wine: Serve this dish with a white Mexican vin ordinaire.

Variation: Whole red snapper is also very tasty broiled. Use 4 cleaned fish and place a sprig of fresh parsley or cilantro in each body cavity. Sprinkle with lemon juice and season with salt and pepper. Broil the red snapper for 10 to 25 minutes, turning once. Serve with Mexican salsa (see page 54).

Tampico-style Salt Cod

Bacalao a la tampicueña

Takes time • Tampico

Serves 4

2 ¼ lb. salt cod
3 medium-sized red bell peppers
1 large onion
2 tbsp. olive oil
6 garlic cloves
2 fresh or canned jalapeño peppers (see Glossary)
freshly ground black pepper
salt
thin lemon wedges for garnish (optional)

Preparation time: 1 hour (plus 25 hours soaking time)

930 cal. per portion

1 Soak the salt cod in plenty of cold water for at least 24 hours, changing the water several times.

2 Preheat the oven to 450 degrees. Cut the bell peppers in half, trim, then lay them cut side downward on a rack, and place in the center of the oven for 15 to 20 minutes, or until the skins are brown and blistered.

3 Remove the peppers from the oven and leave them to cool a little. Remove the skins and seeds and cut the flesh into strips.

4 Peel and finely chop the onion. Heat the oil in a large skillet and fry the onion until transparent. Peel and crush the garlic and add to the onion.

5 Slit the jalapeño peppers along their length, remove the seeds, and cut the peppers into rings. Add the jalapeño chilies and bell peppers to the pan. Pour in ½ cup water, bring to a boil, cover, and cook the vegetables over medium heat for about 5 minutes.

6 Transfer the contents of the pan to a blender or food processor and process to a purée. Return the purée to the pan and bring to a boil. Season the sauce with pepper and a little salt.

7 Remove the salt cod from the water, rinse, remove any remaining bones, and cut into small pieces. Lay the fish in the hot sauce, cover the pan, and cook over medium heat for about 10 minutes.

8 Serve the fish on warmed plates with the sauce poured over the top. Garnish with lemon wedges, if liked.

Marinated Raw Fish

Easy • Acapulco

Ceviche

Serves 4

2 fresh mackerel (about 1 ¼ lb.s)
salt
juice of 6 lemons
2 fresh or canned jalapeño peppers (see Glossary)
1 tbsp. white wine vinegar
1 tsp. dried oregano
4 tbsp. olive oil
2 ½ cups tomatoes
2 small onions
2 ripe avocados

Preparation time: 40 minutes (plus 3 hours marinating time)
860 cal. per portion

1 Skin the fish and carefully detach the flesh from the bones. Cut the fillets into small dice, place them in a shallow bowl, and season lightly with salt.

2 Pour the juice of five of the lemons over the fish, stir thoroughly, cover and leave the diced mackerel to marinate in the refrigerator for about 3 hours.

3 Slit the chili peppers along their length, remove the seeds, and chop the peppers finely. Mix the chili peppers with the vinegar, oregano, and olive oil.

4 Plunge the tomatoes into boiling water, remove the skins and seeds, and finely chop the flesh. Peel the onions. Finely chop 1 onion and stir it into the tomatoes. Cut the other onion into thin rings, and set aside.

5 Remove the fish from the marinade, place it in a large bowl, and stir in the tomato-and-onion mixture. Stir in the chili and herb sauce and mix well. Pile the mackerel mixture in the middle of a large serving platter.

6 Peel the avocados, cut them in half lengthwise, pit each of them, and cut the avocado flesh into long, thin slices. Immediately sprinkle the slices with the rest of the lemon juice to prevent them from discoloring.

7 Arrange the avocado slices with the onion rings to form a border around the fish. Serve immediately.

Salmon and Cilantro Sauce

Easy • Pacific Coast

Salmon en salsa verde

Serves 4

2 green onions (scallions)
½ cup freshly squeezed lime juice
2 fresh or canned jalapeño peppers (see Glossary)
1 small bunch cilantro (about 1 oz.)
5 tbsp. olive oil plus extra for greasing the baking dish
1 lb. 12 oz. salmon fillet, preferably with the skin. (Ask your fishmonger to cut the fish into two equal-sized pieces.)

Preparation time: 30 minutes (plus 40 minutes cooking time)

520 cal. per portion

1 Preheat the oven to 350 degrees. Trim, wash, and finely chop the green onions (scallions). Place them in a small bowl with the lime juice, reserving 1 tbsp. juice for later use.

2 Wash the chili peppers if using fresh, then deseed and finely chop. Wash the cilantro, shake dry, and finely chop the leaves.

3 Add the chilies and cilantro to the green onions (scallions). Add the oil and stir well.

4 Rinse the salmon fillets under cold running water and pat dry. Sprinkle the skinless side of each fillet with the reserved 1 tbsp. lime juice.

5 Lay one fillet, skin side downward, in a greased ovenproof dish, and cover with half the sauce. Place the other fillet on top, skin side upward, with the thicker part of the top fillet over the thin end of the bottom one. Bake the fish, uncovered, in the center of the oven for 25 to 30 minutes.

6 Before serving, remove the skin from the top fillet. Cut the salmon into four portions and serve on warmed plates, with rice and the remaining sauce.

Red Snapper with Oranges

Easy • Pacific Coast

Huachinango en naranjas

Serves 4

2 ¼ lb. red snapper or ocean perch fillets (see Note)
juice of 1 lime
salt
freshly ground black pepper
4 tbsp. butter
1 small onion
3 garlic cloves
1 ¾ cups freshly squeezed orange juice
ground cinnamon
small bunch cilantro or flat-leaved parsley (about 1 oz.)
orange slices for garnish

Preparation time: 1 hour

360 cal. per portion

1 Preheat the oven to 350° degrees. Rinse the fillets or whole fish under cold running water and pat dry. Sprinkle with lime juice and season with salt and pepper. Melt 1 tbsp. of the butter and use to grease a large baking dish, then lay the fish in the dish.

2 Peel and very finely chop the onion. Heat the rest of the butter in a saucepan and fry the onion over low heat until soft.

3 Peel and crush the garlic and add it to the onion with the orange juice and cinnamon. Season with salt and pepper, and simmer, uncovered, for 3 minutes.

4 Pour the hot orange sauce over the fish and bake, uncovered, in the center of the oven for 25 to 30 minutes.

5 Wash the cilantro, shake dry, then tear off the leaves, and finely chop half of them. Wash the orange in hot water, then cut into very thin slices. Remove the dish from the oven. If you are using a whole fish, remove from the dish and fillet it. Return the fish to the dish and sprinkle with the chopped cilantro. Garnish with orange slices, sprinkled with the whole cilantro leaves.

Note: If preferred, cook a whole fish (weighing about 2 lb. 12 oz.) and then fillet it afterward.

Marinated Fish

Pescado en escabeche

Takes time • Guerrero

Serves 4 to 6

3 tbsp. achiote powder (see Glossary, and Note, page 105)
½ cup orange juice
½ cup white wine vinegar
1 tsp. olive oil
2 garlic cloves
¾ cup chicken broth
2 tsp. sugar
4 bayleaves
2¼ lb. fish fillets or fish steaks (for example, halibut, swordfish, red snapper)
vegetable oil for frying
8 oz. red onions

Preparation time: 40 minutes (plus 8 hours marinating time)

210 cal. per portion (if serving 6)

1 In a bowl, mix the achiote powder, 2 tbsp. of the orange juice and 1 tbsp. of the vinegar to a thick paste.

2 Heat the olive oil in a skillet. Peel and crush the garlic, and add it to the oil. Add 2 tbsp. of the paste (see Note) and stir-fry briefly over low heat. Gradually add the remaining orange juice and vinegar, the broth, and the sugar. Add the bayleaves and bring to a boil, then remove the marinade from the heat and set aside.

3 In a large skillet, fry the fish, in batches, in plenty of oil over medium heat for 5 to 7 minutes on each side, until lightly browned.

4 Arrange the fish fillets, side by side, in a shallow dish. Peel the onions, cut them into thin rings, and arrange them over the fish. Pour the marinade over the fish, cover, and leave to marinate in the refrigerator for about 8 hours.

Note: The remaining paste can be stored in the refrigerator and used to brush on other broiled or fried fish.

Serve marinated fish with pickled poblano chili peppers, strips of bell pepper, fresh leaf spinach, and chopped fresh cilantro.

Scallops with Red Peppers

Easy • Campeche

Veiras en salsa roja

Serves 4

2 large red bell peppers
3 garlic cloves
1 fresh medium-hot chili pepper (see Glossary)
2 tbsp. vegetable oil
salt
juice of ½ lime
2 tbsp. heavy cream
1 lb. 5 oz. scallops, shells and coral removed
bunch of cilantro or flat-leaved parsley (1 oz.)
halved lime slices for garnish (optional)

Preparation time: 50 minutes

200 cal. per portion

1 Preheat the oven to 450 degree. Cut the bell peppers in half, trim, then lay them cut side downward on a rack and place in the center of the oven for 15 to 20 minutes, or until the skins are brown and blistered.

2 Meanwhile, peel the garlic. Slit the chili pepper along its length, remove the seeds, then rinse and finely chop the flesh. Heat 1 tbsp. oil in a saucepan and fry the garlic until brown, then add the chopped chili pepper.

3 Remove the peppers from the oven and leave to cool a little. Remove the skins and seeds and cut the flesh into strips. Add to the saucepan and sauté for about 5 minutes. Pour the contents of the pan into a blender and purée, then return the purée to the saucepan. Season with salt and stir in the lime juice and heavy cream. Bring briefly to a boil, then keep warm over low heat.

4 Heat the remaining oil in a skillet and cook the scallops over medium heat for 4 to 5 minutes. Season lightly with salt.

5 Meanwhile, wash the cilantro and shake dry. Reserve a few of the leaves, then chop the rest, and stir them into the sauce. Divide the sauce between four warmed plates and arrange the scallops on top. Sprinkle the reserved cilantro leaves over the top. Garnish with halved lime slices, if wished.

Mexican Shrimp

Easy • Gulf of Mexico

Camarones a la mexicana

Serves 4

1 large onion
4 tbsp. vegetable oil • 3 garlic cloves
2 ¼ cups beefsteak tomatoes
1 fresh medium-hot chili pepper (see Glossary)
salt • freshly ground black pepper
1 bay leaf
½ tsp. dried thyme
small bunch cilantro or flat-leaved parsley (about 1 oz.)
16 large raw, unpeeled shrimp, heads removed
lime juice for sprinkling

Preparation time: 40 minutes

180 cal. per portion

1 Peel and finely chop the onion. Heat 2 tbsp. oil in a skillet and sauté the onion until transparent. Peel and crush the garlic and add it to the onion.

2 Plunge the tomatoes into boiling water, remove the skins and seeds, and finely chop the flesh.

3 Slit the chili pepper along its length, remove the seeds, then rinse well and finely chop the flesh. Add the strips to the pan with the tomatoes and season with salt and pepper.

4 Add the bay leaf and dried thyme. Simmer the mixture, uncovered, for about 10 minutes, until nearly all the liquid has evaporated, then discard the bay leaf. Wash the cilantro, shake dry, and finely chop the leaves.

5 Peel the shrimp. Make an incision along the back of each shrimp and remove the black vein-like intestine. Sprinkle the shrimp with lime juice.

6 Heat the remaining oil in another skillet and fry the shrimp over high heat for 5 to 6 minutes, turning once.

7 Divide the tomato sauce between four plates. Arrange the shrimp on top of the sauce and spoon a little of the sauce over them. Garnish with the chopped cilantro leaves.

Baked Swordfish

Pez espada

Not difficult • Baja California

Serves 4

4 green onions (scallions)
small bunch cilantro or flat-leaved parsley (about 1 oz.)
2 cups beefsteak tomatoes
3 tbsp. olive oil, plus extra for greasing the baking dish
juice of 1 lime
salt
freshly ground black pepper
4 swordfish steaks (about 6 oz. each)

Preparation time: 40 minutes

290 cal. per portion

1 Trim and wash the green onions (scallions), then cut them into thin rings. Rinse the cilantro under cold running water, shake dry, and finely chop the leaves.

2 Plunge the tomatoes into boiling water, remove the skins and seeds, and finely chop the flesh.

3 Preheat the oven to 400 degrees. Grease an oval or rectangular baking dish with oil.

4 In a bowl, combine the green onions (scallions), cilantro, chopped tomatoes, olive oil, and lime juice, and season to taste with salt and pepper.

5 Rinse the fish under cold running water, pat dry, season with salt and pepper, and place side by side in the baking dish. Spread the vegetables over the top, then bake in the center of the oven for 10 to 15 minutes.

Variation: Skin and slice 4 medium-sized tomatoes and spread them on four large pieces of aluminum foil. Lay one swordfish steak on top of each bed of sliced tomato, and sprinkle with chopped garlic and a little cilantro. Sprinkle a little oil over the top, wrap the foil over the fish, and bake in the center of the oven at 400 degrees for 15 to 20 minutes.

Sea Bass in Almond Sauce

Robalo en salsa de almendras

Needs care • Acapulco

Serves 4

4 sea bass fillets (about 7 oz. each)
juice of 1 lemon
salt
freshly ground black pepper
⅔ cup unblanched almonds
1 fresh medium-hot chili pepper (see Glossary)
1 garlic clove • 6 tbsp. sour cream
2 tbsp. vegetable oil plus extra for greasing the baking dish
⅓ cup feta cheese
finely chopped cilantro and small lemon wedges for garnish (optional)

Preparation time: 50 minutes

600 cal. per portion

1 Rinse the sea bass fillets under cold running water and pat dry. Sprinkle the fish on both sides with lemon juice and season with salt and pepper. Cover and leave to stand in the refrigerator for about 30 minutes.

2 Meanwhile, plunge the almonds into boiling water and squeeze them out of their brown skins. Wash and deseed the chili pepper. Peel the garlic.

3 Grind the almonds, chili pepper, garlic, and sour cream in a food processor or a blender. Season the purée with salt and pepper to taste.

4 Preheat the oven to 400 degrees. Heat the oil in a skillet and fry the fillets over medium heat for 2 minutes on each side. Remove the fillets from the pan and arrange them in a greased baking dish.

5 Spread the almond sauce evenly over the fish and grate the feta cheese over the top. Place the dish in the center of the oven and bake the fish for about 10 minutes, until the cheese begins to melt and turn light brown.

6 Serve the fish at once. Garnish with finely chopped cilantro and lemon wedges, if liked.

Sauza
EXTRA
HECHO EN MEXICO

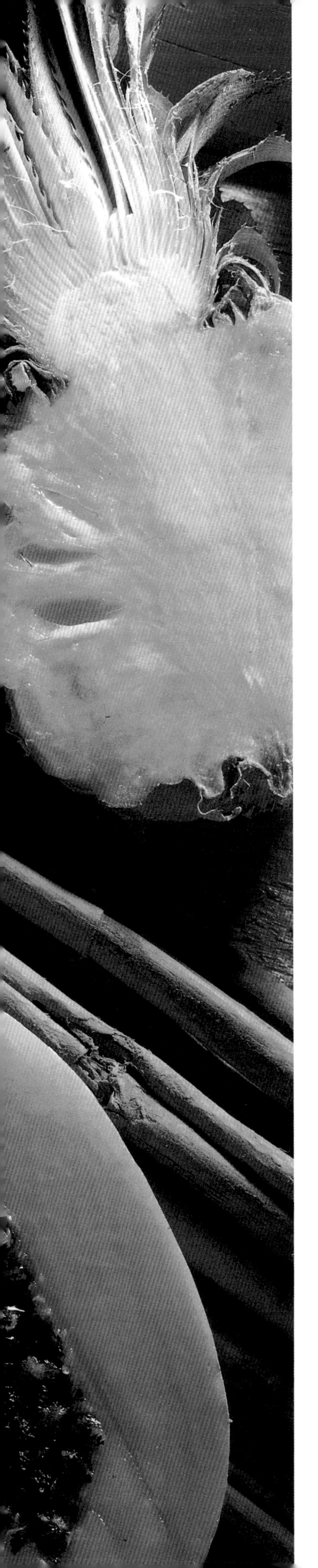

DESSERTS, PASTRIES, AND DRINKS

In pre-Hispanic times, the Mexican Indians ended their meals with aromatic, sweet-tasting papayas and mangoes, juicy pineapples, melons, bananas, citrus fruits, coconuts, and a myriad of other exotic fruits. Fruit is still a favorite dessert, on its own or transformed into delicious hot baked dishes, fruit sponge puddings, chilled mousses, and refreshing sherbets.

The Spaniards introduced some of their own recipes to Mexico, many of which, especially those using lots of egg yolks and sugar, were invented in convent kitchens. Among the first people to be inspired by these recipes were the nuns of Puebla, who created the thick, creamy egg liqueur known as *rompope*, which can be poured over puddings or fruit or, like *licor de café*, served as an after-dinner drink.

For their many feast days, Mexicans bake special cakes and pastries such as *rosca de reyes*, a ring of yeast-raised pastry made to celebrate the Epiphany, and *pan de muertos*, Bread of the Dead, eaten on the Day of the Dead, Catholic All Souls' Day in early November. This sweet bread is usually decorated with a skull and crossbones.

Sweet, spicy coffee or hot chocolate are the usual accompaniments to sweet bread or cakes; chocolate drinks were for many years reserved for the privileged rich, for cocoa beans were regarded as a gift from the gods.

Coconut Dessert

More complicated • Puebla

Cocada

Serves 4

1 small coconut
1 cup milk
½ cup heavy cream
½ cup sugar
4 egg yolks
5 tbsp. white rum
butter or vegetable oil for greasing the dish
1 tsp. ground cinnamon
5 tbsp. blanched, halved almonds

Preparation time: 1 hour (plus 25 minutes cooking time and 1 hour for cooling)

420 cal. per portion

1 Use a corkscrew to gouge out the "eyes" of the coconut (*above*) and pour the coconut water inside into a small saucepan. Wrap the coconut in a kitchen towel and break the shell with a hammer.

2 Remove the coconut flesh from the shell and peel away the thin brown skin with a sharp knife or vegetable peeler (see *above*). Rinse the coconut flesh briefly under cold running water, dry, and grate it fairly coarsely with a vegetable greater.

3 Add the milk, cream, and sugar to the liquid in the pan and bring slowly to a boil. Stir in the grated coconut, cover and simmer the mixture over low heat for about 25 minutes, stirring from time to time. Remove the pan from the heat and leave the contents to cool a little. Meanwhile, preheat to oven to 450 degrees.

4 Mix the egg yolks and rum in a bowl, then stir them into the coconut mixture. Simmer over low heat until the mixture thickens, stirring frequently.

5 Grease on ovenproof dish and pour in the coconut mixture. Smooth the top with the back of a spoon, sprinkle the ground cinnamon over the dessert, and decorate with the almond halves. Bake on the top shelf of the oven for about 10 minutes, until brown to top.

6 Allow the dessert to cool a little before cutting it into small squares. Serve warm or cold.

Note: When buying a coconut, make sure you shake it. The more liquid it contains, the fresher it is.

To make opening the coconut easier, preheat the oven to 400 degrees. Gouge out two of the three "eyes" in the coconut, using a corkscrew or screwdriver, and drain out the liquid. Place the empty coconut in the oven for about 15 minutes, then place it on a chopping board and break it into pieces with a hammer.

If preferred, you can use 2 to 2 ½ cups ready grated coconut, but bear in mind you will also need ½ to 1 cup coconut liquid.

Almond Milk Pudding

Flan de almendras

Takes time • Morelos

Serves 4 to 6

1 cup sugar
1 ¼ cups milk
¾ cup heavy cream
⅔ cup blanched, finely ground almonds
6 eggs

Preparation time: 1 hour (plus 12 hours chilling time)

480 cal. per portion (if serving 6)

1 Preheat the oven to 350 degrees. Melt 6 tbsp. of the sugar in a saucepan with 1 tbsp. water, over medium heat, stirring, until it forms a light brown caramel. Pour the caramel into a 10-inch baking dish or tube pan, tipping the dish or pan from side to side so that the caramel coats the base and sides of the dish.

2 Heat the milk and cream in a small saucepan. Add the rest of the sugar and continue to cook over low heat until the sugar has dissolved. Remove the pan from the heat and stir in the almonds.

3 Whisk the eggs in a bowl. Add 4 tbsp. of the almond and milk mixture, then stir the eggs into the milk, using an egg whisk. Pour into the baking dish. Place the dish in a roasting pan in the center of the oven, and fill the pan with boiling water to a level of about 1 inch. Bake the pudding in this bain-marie for about 40 minutes. If the top starts to brown too much, cover it with aluminum foil.

4 Remove the baking dish from the bain-marie and leave to cool, then chill in the refrigerator for at least 3 hours, or preferably overnight.

5 To unmold the pudding, draw the tip of a knife around the rim of the baking dish or tube pan to loosen the edge. Dip the baking dish into hot water for 2 to 3 seconds, if necessary. Place a moistened serving plate on top of the baking dish or tube pan, then quickly invert them both, giving the pan several sharp taps and shakes. Leave the baking dish or tube pan upturned for a few minutes to allow the caramel to drain out, and then serve.

Mangoes with Coffee Liqueur

Takes time • Colimo

Mangos con licor de café

Serves 4

For the liqueur:
2 pieces cinnamon stick, 1 ½ and 3 inches
⅔ cup brown sugar
5 tbsp. freshly ground coffee
1 tsp. vanilla sugar (see Glossary)
6 egg yolks
½ cup evaporated milk
5 tbsp. evaporated or heavy cream
1 cup rum (54 proof)

For the dessert:
2 medium-sized ripe mangoes
½ cup whipping cream

Preparation time: 1 hour (plus 3 hours chilling time)

430 cal. per portion

1 For the liqueur, bring 1 cup water to a boil in a saucepan with the two cinnamon sticks and 3 tbsp. of the sugar. Cover and simmer over medium heat for about 5 minutes. Add the coffee and return to a boil. Remove the pan from the heat and allow the hot coffee to stand for about 5 minutes, then strain through a fine sieve and leave to cool.

2 Meanwhile, grind the remaining sugar to a powder in a blender. Mix the powdered sugar and the vanilla sugar in a metal bowl. Add the egg yolks and beat with an egg whisk until creamy.

3 Place the bowl over a saucepan of gently simmering water and continue to whisk over low heat until the egg yolk mixture thickens. Remove the bowl from the saucepan and stir in the evaporated milk, cream, rum and, finally, the cool coffee-and-cinnamon mixture.

4 Rinse out a 3-cup to 1-quart bottle with hot water. Pour the coffee liqueur into the bottle. Seal, allow to cool, then chill in the refrigerator for 2 to 3 hours.

5 To make the dessert, peel each of the mangoes, remove the pit, and cut the flesh lengthwise into wedges. Whip the whipping cream until stiff.

6 Arrange the mangoes on four serving plates. Pour the coffee liqueur over the mangoes and add a dollop of whipped cream at the side of each plate.

Note: The liqueur will keep in the refrigerator for up to six months. It is delicious with ice cream or desserts, or it can be served "straight" as a drink.

MAYA

Bread of the Dead

Takes time • All regions

Pan de muertos

Make 1 loaf (8 to 12 slices)

6 tbsp. milk
2 tbsp. butter
6 tbsp. sugar
½ tsp. salt • 1 tsp. aniseed
freshly grated nutmeg
1 ½ tbsp. fresh yeast or 1 package active dry yeast
2 eggs, one of them separated
4 cups all-purpose flour
2 tsp. sugar for sprinkling
½ tsp. ground cinnamon

Preparation time: 30 minutes (plus 2 hours proving time and 30 minutes baking time)

200 cal. per slice (if serving 12)

1 Heat the milk until lukewarm. Cut the butter into flakes and add to the milk with the sugar, the salt, aniseed, and nutmeg. Leave to cool. Crumble the fresh yeast (or sprinkle the dried yeast) into a bowl and mix with 6 tbsp. lukewarm water. Cover and leave for about 5 minutes. Add the milk mixture, the egg and egg yolk and all but 2 tbsp. of the flour. Work to a dough with the dough hook attachment of a mixer. Cover and leave to rise for 1 ½ hours.

2 Knead the dough vigorously, adding more all-purpose flour if it is too soft. Grease a cookie sheet. Reserve a little dough for decoration and shape the rest into a round loaf. Place on the cookie sheet.

3 Shape the reserved dough into shapes of teardrops and an even number of long bone shapes, and leave to prove on the cookie sheet for a further 30 minutes.

4 Preheat the oven to 400 degrees. Whisk the egg white and use to brush the loaf. Brush the underside of the teardrops and bones with egg white. Cross each pair of bones, then place on the loaf with the teardrops and press gently.

5 Bake in the center of the oven for 30 to 35 minutes, until golden-brown. If the decorations brown too quickly, cover with aluminum foil. Leave to cool. Mix the 2 tsp. sugar with the cinnamon and sprinkle over the loaf.

Nutty Bread Pudding

Bread for Lent • Sinaloa

Capirotada

Serves 6 to 8

For the syrup:
½ cup sugar
1 tsp. ground cinnamon
½ cup milk

For the pudding:
6 tbsp. butter plus extra for greasing the baking dish
12 to 14 slices white sandwich loaf
⅔ cup chopped walnuts
⅔ cup unsalted, shelled peanuts
⅔ cup raisins
1 ½ cups mozzarella cheese

Preparation time: 40 minutes (plus 40 minutes baking time)

520 cal. (if serving 8)

1 To make the syrup, boil 1 cup water and the sugar in a small saucepan for about 20 minutes, stirring constantly. Add the cinnamon and milk, and set aside.

2 Preheat the oven to 450 degrees. Melt the butter and use half to grease a cookie sheet. Spread out the sliced bread on the cookie sheet and sprinkle it with the rest of the melted butter. Bake in the center of the oven for about 10 minutes, until the bread is golden, turning once.

3 Reduce the heat to 325 degrees. Grease an ovenproof baking dish and line with half the bread slices. Sprinkle with one third of the syrup.

4 Mix together the walnuts, peanuts, and raisins. Chop the mozzarella into small dice. Sprinkle half the raisin-and-nut mixture and half the cheese over the bread in the dish.

5 Lay the rest of the bread on the top. Sprinkle with the rest of the syrup and cover with the remaining raisins, nuts, and cheese. Bake in the center of the oven for 35 to 40 minutes, until the pudding is crisp on top. Serve straight from the oven, or leave until cold.

Note: Every Mexican region has its own version of this delicious bread pudding, which is traditionally eaten during Lent.

Golden Pineapple

More complex • Puebla

Piña dorada

Serves 4

1 large, ripe pineapple
3 tbsp. butter
2 tbsp. brown sugar
2 tbsp. rum
¾ cup heavy cream
2 tbsp. superfine sugar
1 egg
1 egg yolk
2 tbsp. cornstarch
1 tsp. vanilla sugar (see Glossary)
salt
a few mint leaves for garnish (optional)

Preparation time: 45 minutes

450 cal. per portion

1 Preheat the oven to 400 degrees. Rinse the pineapple under cold running water and pat dry. Cut off the top third. Cut the flesh away from the rest to make a hollow shell (*above*) and cut the flesh from the top third.

2 Using a spoon or a melon baller, scoop out the flesh, taking care not to damage the shell (see *above*).

3 Chop the pineapple flesh into small chunks, discarding the woody core.

4 Place the chunks in a bowl. Cut the butter into small dice and add it to the pineapple with the brown sugar and the rum, and stir thoroughly.

5 Fill the hollow shell with the mixture and place it in an overproof dish. Bake on the lower shelf of the oven for about 30 minutes.

6 Meanwhile, place the cream, caster sugar, egg, and egg yolk in a small saucepan. Mix the cornstarch with a little cold water in a bowl or cup, then pour it into the pan. Stir in the vanilla sugar and little salt.

7 Heat the sauce slowly over low heat, stirring constantly, and simmer until it begins to thicken. Remove the pan from the heat and leave the sauce to cool.

8 Remove the pineapple from the oven. Pour a little of the sauce over the pineapple chunks and serve the rest separately. Decorate the pineapple and the sauce with a few mint leaves before serving, if wished.

Note: When choosing a pineapple, look for one with firm, fleshy looking green leaves – a leaf pulled gently from the center should come away easily. A ripe pineapple should have a fragrant smell and feel slightly soft to the touch.

For added color when serving this dish, the pineapple shell is decorated with a hibiscus flower. You can choose from a selection of other edible flowers, such as roses, nasturtiums, marigolds, or violets.

Variation: Use four miniature pineapples, which look very attractive and are just the right size for a single serving.

Epiphany Ring

Rosca de reyes

Takes time • All regions

Serves 6 to 8

4 cups all-purpose flour
1 ½ tbsp. fresh yeast or 1 package active dry yeast
2 tbsp. sugar
7 tbsp. butter plus extra for greasing the cookie sheet
3 eggs
3 egg yolks
grated rind of ½ untreated lemon
salt
3 tbsp. finely chopped candied lemon peel
⅔ cup finely chopped candied fruits
sugar for sprinkling (optional)

Preparation time: 30 minutes (plus 50 minutes proving time and 30 minutes baking time)

450 cal. per portion

1 Sift the flour into a bowl and make a well in the center. Crumble the fresh yeast and mix it with the 2 tbsp. sugar and 4 tbsp. warm water (or mix in the dried yeast, if using) and pour into the well in the flour. Cover and leave for about 20 minutes.

2 Melt the butter over low heat. In a bowl, mix together the 3 eggs and 2 of the egg yolks, the melted butter, lemon rind, and a little salt, then add to the yeast mixture in the other bowl. Using the dough hook attachment of a hand mixer, mix to a smooth dough.

3 Knead the candied lemon peel and candied fruits into the dough. Grease a cookie sheet. Briefly knead the dough again and then shape it into a ring. Place the ring on the prepared cookie sheet, cover, and leave to prove for about 30 minutes. Meanwhile, preheat the oven to 350 degrees.

4 Beat the remaining egg yolk and brush it over the surface of the cake. Bake in the center of the oven for about 30 minutes. Leave the cake to cool on a wire rack, then sprinkle with another 2 tbsp. sugar, if desired.

Note: This bread is traditionally eaten on January 6th, also called Twelfth Night, Epiphany, or the Feast of Kings. Often, a small doll is pressed into the cooked cake from the underside; the person who finds the doll is required to throw a party on Candlemas day, February 2nd.

Almond Cookies

Takes time • Puebla

Polverones de almendras

Makes about 50

1 ½ cups butter or lard plus extra for greasing the cookie sheet
1 ¾ cups powdered sugar
1 egg yolk
1 tsp. vanilla extract
⅔ cup blanched, finely ground almonds
3 ½ cups all-purpose flour
salt

Preparation time: 40 minutes (plus 1 ½ hours baking time)

110 cal. per cookie

1 Allow the butter or lard to soften, then whisk by hand until frothy. Gradually blend in 2 tsp. of the powdered sugar, the egg yolk, vanilla, almonds, all-purpose flour, and a little salt.

2 Preheat the oven to 300 degrees. Grease a cookie sheet. Shape the dough into walnut-sized balls (rinsing your hands frequently under cold running water). Arrange half of them on the cookie sheet, about ¼ inch apart.

3 Bake in the center of the oven for about 45 minutes. The cookies should still be a pale color.

4 Transfer the cookies to a wire rack and leave until not quite cold.

5 Meanwhile, bake the remaining dough balls the same way and cool on the wire rack.

6 Sift the remaining powdered sugar onto a plate. Turn the cookies in the powdered sugar and return them to the rack, then sift a generous quantity of powdered sugar over them so that they are covered with a snowy-white layer.

Layered Fruit Dessert

Time consuming • Puebla

Ante de frutas

Serves 6 to 8

For the sponge:
8 eggs
½ cup sugar
1 ¼ cups cornstarch • 3 tbsp. fine cornmeal
1 tbsp. baking powder • ½ cup butter
grated rind of 1 untreated lemon

For the syrup:
⅔ cup brown sugar
2 inch piece cinnamon stick
¾ cup medium sherry

For the fruit purée:
3 cups peaches
2 cups blanched almonds
6 tbsp. honey
8 gelatin leaves or 2 tbsp. powdered gelatin

lemon leaves (optional)

Preparation time: 2 hours (plus 1 ½ hours for chilling)

690 cal. per portion (if serving 8)

1 Preheat the oven to 375 degrees. Separate the eggs. Whisk the yolks with the sugar in a bowl until creamy. In a separate bowl, whisk the whites until stiff, then fold them into the yolks. Mix the cornstarch, cornmeal, and baking powder and sift into the eggs. Carefully mix all the ingredients. Melt the butter in a saucepan, then fold the butter and the lemon rind into the sponge mixture.

2 Grease a 10 by 12 inch cake pan and sprinkle with a little flour. Pour in the sponge mixture, and bake in the center of the oven for 25 minutes, or until well risen. Unmold the sponge from the pan and leave to cool on a wire rack.

3 To make the syrup, boil ¾ cup water in a pan with the brown sugar and cinnamon stick for about 10 minutes. Strain through a sieve and stir in the sherry. To make the purée, plunge the peaches into boiling water, then peel, halve, and pit them. Reserve about 25 almonds, and purée the remainder with the peaches and honey in a food processor or blender.

4 Soak the gelatin according to the instructions on the package. Heat the fruit purée, squeeze out the gelatin, stir it into the purée, and continue to stir until it dissolves. Pour into a bowl and leave to set in the refrigerator for about 30 minutes.

5 Cut the sponge in half horizontally. Sprinkle the cut surfaces with syrup. Spread half the purée over one half of the sponge. Place the other sponge on top and spread it with the rest of the purée. Cut into six to eight portions. Halve the almonds and arrange them in a pattern on top of each portion. Chill in the refrigerator for at least 1 hour before serving. Decorate the serving dish with lemon leaves, if liked.

Note: 2 tbsp. powdered gelatin can be substituted for the leaf gelatin.

Bananas with Hot Pineapple

Quick • Michoacán

Plátanos con piña

Serves 4

1 small fresh pineapple
3 tbsp. butter
2 tbsp. sugar
4 tbsp. white rum
4 small bananas
juice of 1 lemon
grated chocolate for decoration

Preparation time: 45 minutes

260 cal. per portion

1 Remove the crest of leaves from the pineapple and peel carefully. Cut the pineapple lengthwise into quarters and remove the hard core. Halve the pieces lengthwise and chop the pineapple into smaller chunks.

2 Melt the butter in a saucepan over low heat. Add the sugar and stir until it dissolves. Stir in the pineapple and rum, and cook for about 5 minutes, stirring.

3 Peel the bananas, cut them in half lengthwise, and arrange them on four individual serving dishes. Sprinkle the bananas with lemon juice so that they do not discolor.

4 Pour the hot pineapple and rum sauce over the bananas. Sprinkle with grated chocolate and serve at once, decorated with a few leaves from the crest of the pineapple, if wished.

Oranges with Mousse Filling

Easy • Nuevo León

Naranjas rellenas

Serves 4

4 large oranges (see Note)
about 1 ½ cup white wine
4 tbsp. sugar
6 leaves gelatin or 1 tbsp. powdered gelatin
1 egg
8 cherries and mint leaves for decoration

Preparation time: 40 minutes

(plus 2 ½ hours for chilling)
220 cal. per portion

1 Cut the oranges in half crosswise and carefully squeeze out all the juice (do not damage the shell). Using a teaspoon, scrape away the remaining fruit. Reserve the hollow orange halves.

2 Measure the orange juice and top up with white wine to make 2 cups. Stir in the sugar, then warm the mixture in a saucepan, but do not allow it to boil.

3 Soak the gelatin according to the instructions on the package and squeeze out. Stir the gelatin into the orange juice and continue beating with a hand whisk until dissolved. Remove the pan from the heat and leave to cool.

4 Separate the egg. Whisk the yolk into the lukewarm orange juice. Cool a little more, then place it in the refrigerator for 20 to 30 minutes, until it begins to set. Whisk the egg white until stiff, then fold it into the gelatin mixture.

5 Spoon the mousse into the orange halves and chill in the refrigerator for about 2 hours, until firmly set. Before serving, decorate with cherries and a few mint leaves.

Note: If possible, use large, sweet Navel oranges, which have few, if any, seeds.

Egg Liqueur with Fruit Salad

Special occasion dessert • Puebla

Rompope

(Serves 4 to 6)

Makes 1 quart egg liqueur
1 quart milk
⅔ cup sugar
1 vanilla pod
6 cloves
¾ cup freshly ground almonds
12 egg yolks
1 cup rum

For the fruit salad:
1 papaya, 1 mango, 1 medium-sized pineapple and ½ small melon

Preparation time: 1 hour

600 cal. per portion (if serving 6)

1 Place the milk, sugar, vanilla pod, cloves, and almonds in a saucepan and bring to a boil. Simmer over low heat for 5 minutes. Remove the pan from the heat and leave the milk to stand for about 10 minutes, stirring from time to time to prevent a skin forming. Discard the vanilla pod and cloves.

2 In a bowl, whisk the egg yolks until they are thick and frothy. Slowly stir in ½ cup of the almond milk.

3 Stir the egg yolk mixture, a little at a time, into the almond milk. Warm the milk mixture in the pan over medium heat, or pour it into a heatproof bowl set over a saucepan of simmering water, and then stir constantly with a wooden spoon, until the mixture begins to thicken and it coats the back of the spoon. Do not allow the sauce to boil, otherwise the eggs will curdle.

4 Remove the pan from the heat and stir in the rum. Pour the liqueur into a clean bottle, seal it and leave to cool.

5 To serve, peel the papaya, mango and pineapple, and cut them into small chunks. Deseed the melon and scoop out the flesh with a melon-baller. Mix the fruit in a serving dish and pour the egg liqueur over the top.

Note: The egg liqueur can be served as a drink in a small glass, sprinkled with freshly grated nutmeg, or as a sauce with fruit salad, ice cream, or puddings.

Use very fresh eggs from a reliable source for this recipe, in order to reduce the risk of salmonella. Although the risk is small, "at risk" people – including the very young, the elderly or sick, and pregnant women – should avoid raw or very lightly cooked eggs.

Pot Coffee

Quick • All regions

Café de olla

Serves 4

1 x 3-inch cinnamon stick • 3 cloves
⅔ cup piloncillo or brown sugar (see Note, recipe below)
1 tsp. grated orange rind
8 tbsp. coarsely ground coffee

Preparation time: 15 minutes

100 cal. per portion

1 Bring 3 cups water to a boil in a small saucepan or an earthenware pot with the cinnamon stick and cloves, then simmer for about 10 minutes.

2 Add the sugar and orange rind, and continue to simmer until the sugar has completely dissolved. Sprinkle the coffee into the water and simmer for a further 3 minutes. Remove the pan from the heat, cover, and leave to infuse until the coffee settles. Strain through a sieve and serve.

Note: This coffee is traditionally made and served in handleless earthenware pots – hence its name.

Hot Chocolate

Easy • All regions

Campurrado

Serves 4

6 tbsp. masa harina (see Glossary)
2 tbsp. piloncillo or brown sugar (see Note)
8 cm piece cinnamon stick
7 oz. unsweetened chocolate

Preparation time: 25 minutes

380 cal. per portion

1 Mix the masa harina with 1 quart water and stir until it has completely dissolved. Strain the liquid through a sieve into a saucepan and bring to simmering point with the brown sugar and cinnamon over medium heat.

2 Finely grate the chocolate and add to the hot masa mixture. Simmer, stirring, until the chocolate has melted. Serve the hot chocolate immediately.

Note: Instead of masa harina, your can use 1 cup whipping cream mixed with 3 cups milk, or 1 quart milk, but the result will not be quite the same.

In Mexico, *piloncillo* sugar, a crude brown sugar, sold in the shape of a little cone, is traditionally used to sweeten this chocolate drink. Raw sugar is the best substitute.

You can use sweet Mexican chocolate (see Glossary) for this recipe, but reduce the quantity of sugar.

Fruit Drink

Quick • All regions

Agua fresca

Serves 4

1 cantaloupe or Persian melon
3 to 4 tbsp. sugar
juice of 1 lemon
2 cups ice-cold, still mineral water
ice cubes

Preparation time: 15 minutes

180 cal. per portion

1 Cut the melon first in half, then into quarters, then into eighths. Remove the seeds and skin, then cut the flesh into large chunks.

2 Place the melon chunks, sugar, and lemon juice in a food processor or blender and purée them.

3 Pour the melon purée into a jug, top up with the mineral water, and stir in a few ice cubes. Serve immediately.

Note: This drink can be made with all sorts of different fruits. Kiwi fruits and raspberries are particularly delicious served in this way.

CERVECERIA MODELO

Fruit and Wine Punch

Simple • All regions

Sangria

Makes 4 to 6 glasses

juice of 3 limes • juice of 3 oranges
3 cups dry red wine
4 cl orange-flavored liqueur
3 to 5 tbsp. sugar, according to taste
1 untreated orange
2 peaches
½ fresh pineapple

Preparation time: 20 minutes (plus 1 hour chilling time)

190 cal. per glass (if serving 6 glasses)

1 Pour the lime juice, orange juice, red wine, and orange-flavored liqueur into a punch bowl or jug, add the sugar to taste and stir thoroughly.

2 Rinse the orange under hot running water and wipe dry. Slice thinly, then cut the slices in half and add them to the punch.

3 Wash and pit the peaches and cut them into small pieces. Peel the half pineapple and cut the flesh into small chunks. Add the peaches and pineapple to the punch bowl or jug.

4 Cover and chill in the refrigerator for at least 1 hour before serving.

Note: This deliciously refreshing drink was brought to the New World from Spain and has become extremely popular throughout Mexico.

Add some ice cubes to the punch bowl before serving, if wished.

Tequila Cocktail

Easy • Jalisco

Margarita

Makes 4 glasses

juice of 3 limes • 1 ¼ cups tequila
3 tsp. orange-flavored liqueur
salt for the rims of the glasses
8 tbsp. crushed ice

Preparation time: 10 minutes

100 cal. per glass

1 Mix together the lime juice, tequila, and orange-flavored liqueur in a cocktail shaker or blender.

2 Sprinkle the salt onto a plate. Briefly dip four upturned cocktail glasses first into cold water, then into the salt on the plate, to create a ¼-inch wide border of salt all round the rims of the glasses (this adds a wonderful piquant edge to the cocktail).

3 Fill the glasses with crushed ice and pour the cocktail mixture over the ice. Serve at once.

Tomato and Orange Drink

Spicy • All regions

Sangrita

Makes 4 glasses

2 oranges • 1 lime
1 cup tomato juice
cayenne pepper
4 green onions (scallions)

Preparation time: 10 minutes

15 cal. per glass

1 Squeeze the oranges and lime. Mix the fruit juice with the tomato juice and then season the drink generously with cayenne pepper.

2 Trim and wash the green onions (scallions), leaving on ½ to 2 inches of the green part.

3 Pour the tomato and orange drink into the glasses and stand 1 green onion (scallion) in each glass.

Note: If wished, place a few ice cubes in the glasses, pour the drink over the top and add the green onions (scallions).

Suggested Menus

Mexicans generally eat several small meals a day, mealtimes being similar to those in Spain – probably a legacy of the conquistadors. The day begins with *desayuno*, an early breakfast taken between 5 and 7 o'clock in the morning which may just consist of only fresh fruit juice or coffee and bread. The substantial second breakfast, *almuerzo*, eaten between 9 and 11 a.m., resembles what we would call brunch. For Mexicans, it is "el que da las energás para el día," the meal that provides energy for the day, and rightly so, since it consists of eggs served in various ways, beans, tortillas, chilaquiles or enchiladas. Lunch (*comida*) takes place from 2.30 p.m. onward; the menu includes a liquid or dry soup, a fish or meat entrée, salad or vegetables, dessert, and coffee.

Between 6 and 7 p.m. in the evening, the family meets at home for *merienda*, afternoon tea, consisting of coffee, tea, or hot chocolate with pastries or cakes. The evening meal is sometimes very light, sometimes a full menu, as at midday. Mexicans love to eat out, so *cena*, dinner, is often enjoyed away from home with friends, work colleagues or family. The meal begins with a margarita, accompanied by cocktail snacks (*botanas*) such as almonds, chicarrones, or olives. Then come the *antojitos*, or appetizers, small dishes, and tortillas of all kinds, followed by a several-course menu. Tex-mex cuisine, which includes dishes such as chili con carne and stuffed taco shells, is delicious but is not traditional Mexican cooking, and for this reason those recipes are not included in this book.

Fresh fruit or ice-cream is suggested for dessert in some of the menus. Since no recipes for these appear in the book, they are marked with an *; this also applies to such accompaniments as fresh bread, and drinks such as tequila.

Quick and easy menus

Menus to prepare in advance

Vegetarian menus

Hot weather menus

Substantial meals for cold days

Chicken Tostadas	32
Chorizo Soup	61
Ragout of Pork with Capers	94
Fried Chayote	75
Cheese Enchiladas	31
Mushroom Soup	64
Baked Swordfish	117
Avocado Dip with Cauliflower	57
Almond Milk Pudding	122
Cheese Quesadillas (variation)	36
Spicy Bean Stew	60
Fresh Mangoes*	—
Red Chilaquiles	37
Veracruz-style Fish Soup	63
Pork with Fruit	93
Fruit Salad*	—

Meals for picnics

Marinated Turkey	104
Pork Tamales	34
Avocado Salad	41
Tomato Salad	42
Fish Salad	46
Sausages in Corn Husks	49
Avocado Dip with Tortilla Chips	57
Pineapple and Papaya Salad	42
Sweetcorn Gratin	84
Almond Cookies	129
Fresh fruit, such as melon*	—

Mexican fiesta

In Mexico, there is always something being celebrated somewhere. Here are a few easy-to-follow suggestions, perfect for a brunch.

Exotic fruit platter* (Pineapple, papayas, mangoes, and bananas, peeled and sliced and arranged on a dish)	—
Avocado Salad	41
Fish Salad	46
Mexican Scrambled Eggs	48
Avocado Dip with Tortilla Chips	57
Sausages in Corn Husks	49
Almond Milk Pudding	122
Cornmeal Tortillas	26
or Wheat Tortillas	28
Pot Coffee	134
Hot Chocolate	134
Tea and freshly squeezed fruit juices*	—
Fresh bread*	—

Tortilla party

When your guests arrive, you may like to welcome them with a margarita or tequila, served in traditional style with salt and lemon. Then simply prepare lots of tortillas and a variety of different fillings and salsas to the everyone can help themselves to as much as they please.

Squid and bean salad	45
Tomato salad	42
Cornmeal Tortillas	26
or Wheat Tortillas	28
with Beef Filling, see recipe for Tacos with Beef Filling	29
Vegetable Filling, see recipe for Burritos with vegetables	31
Chicken filling, see recipe for Chicken Tostadas	32
Refried Beans	80
Avocado Dip	57
Red Bean Sauce	54
Coconut Dessert	120
Egg Liqueur with Fruit Salad	133

Mexican buffet

Chilled Avocado Soup	70
Marinated Turkey	104
Marinated Raw Fish	110
Marinated Fish	113
Sweet Potatoes with Tequila	76
Green Beans with Limes	87
Sausages in Corn Husks	49
Almond Cookies	129
Nutty Bread Pudding	125
Coconut Dessert	120
Mangoes with Coffee Liqueur	123
Fruit Salad*	—

Easter Menu

Since most Mexicans are devout Catholics, they eat no meat during Lent. Easter is always celebrated with large gatherings of family and friends.

Burritos with Vegetables	31
Cheese Enchiladas	31
Red Bean Sauce	54
Cooked Chili Sauce	54
Tomato Salad	42
Fish Salad	46
Cream of Sweetcorn Soup	67
Rice with Pomegranate	83
Scallops with Red Peppers	114
Mexican Shrimp	114
Layered Fruit Dessert	130
Egg Liqueur with Fruit Salad	133
Pot Coffee	134

Glossary

This glossary is intended as a brief guide to some less familiar cooking terms and ingredients, including words and items found on Mexican menus.

Achiote: the seed of the tropical annatto or lipstick trees (bixa orellana). When the seeds are boiled in water, they give off a dye that colors food a bright yellow to reddish color. Achiote is mainly used in the cooking of the Yucatán peninsula. It is sold in powdered form and can, if necessary, be replaced by saffron or sweet paprika.

Agave: a plant whose sap is fermented to make tequila. See also page 76.

Almendras: almonds, the pits of the peach-like fruit of the almond tree, which flourishes in Mexico's hot climate. Ground, chopped or whole almonds are a popular dessert ingredient.

Almuerzo: a hearty second breakfast, consisting of substantial dishes made from such ingredients as eggs, and refried or whole beans.

Ante: a rich dessert made with sponge cake and syrup.

Antojitos: literally translated, the word means "little whims." In Mexico, it is the name given to the many small snacks, such as tortillas and their many variations, available everywhere from street-corner stalls to luxury restaurants.

Arroz: rice, served almost daily in a variety of ways as sopa seca, "dry soup," before the main course.

Atole: a drink of Indian origin, made from masa (cornmeal dough) mixed with water, puréed fruit, herbs, and other flavorings.

Botanos: little nibbles, ranging from almonds, potato chips, or olives to tamales and all kinds of tortillas, always served with drinks in Mexico.

Budín: a kind of baked dessert.

Cacahuates: peanuts. Roasted and salted, they are enjoyed with apéritifs. For some dishes, they are ground and used to make sauces.

Café de olla: coffee made and served in an earthenware pot, with cinnamon and piloncillo sugar.

Café: coffee. The coffee plant was first brought to Mexico in the early 19th century. It has since been cultivated in the coastal regions, and about 60 percent of the harvest is exported. Mexican city-dwellers cannot do without a cup of coffee after lunch. Café de olla is served in the countryside.

Calabacitas: little squash, usually zucchini squash, a favorite vegetable in Mexico. Squash blossoms (flor de calabaza) are used in soups and sauces, or served stuffed.

Camote: the sweet potato, also known as batata, native to Central and South America. Batatas are plants whose roots thicken to form potato-like tubers. Sometimes round, sometimes long and pointed, the tubers have a reddish skin and pale yellow to bright orange flesh. Despite its name, the sweet potato is not related to the potato.

Canela: cinnamon. In Mexican cuisine, both cinnamon sticks and ground cinnamon are used in savoury dishes, and to flavor desserts and drinks.

Cena: lavish hot evening meal which consists of several courses.

Ceviche: raw fish or seafood, marinated in plenty of lime juice and served cold.

Charales: small, white, almost transparent fish, usually sold dried.

Chayote: a pear-shaped squash with pale yellow to green skin. The flavor is similar to that of zucchini.

Chicharron: seasoned pork rind, cut into pieces, and dried. It is fried until crisp and crunchy, and is a popular cocktail snack. It is also cooked in chili sauce, used as a taco filling, or as a garnish.

Chili peppers: these are a traditional ingredient in Mexican cooking, giving characteristic flavor to many dishes. In the southern part of central Mexico, they have been grown since 6000 BC, making them one of the oldest cultivated plants in the land. The chili peppers listed below are a small selection of the most popular types used in Mexican cooking. If you are unable to find a particular one, you can use medium-hot Italian or Turkish chili peppers, or the hotter Far Eastern type. Many Mexican dishes are hot – you may prefer to use less than the suggested amount of chili peppers to begin with. Lovers of really fiery food should not remove the seeds, since they contain most of the spicy substances. Discard the seeds if you prefer a milder taste.
Warning: Chili peppers contain volatile oils that can irritate the skin and eyes, and must be handled with caution. Your should wash your hands immediately after handling them.

Anaheim: a mild, green chili pepper, available fresh. Large enough to stuff.
Ancho: a dried, dark red variety of the poblano chili. Mexicans regard it as one of the milder sort, but it is still very hot.
Caribe: a mild, sweet, yellow chili, available fresh. It can be eaten raw in salads and sauces.
Chipotle: a dried, smoked jalapeño pepper. Use sparingly; it is extremely hot.
Guajillo: a long, narrow, red, and fairly hot pepper. Used dried in cooking it is either soaked before use, or roasted and then finely ground.
Güero: a long, yellow chili pepper. It is hot, with a distinctive flavor.
Habanero: an extremely hot orange chili with a fruity flavor. Available fresh.
Jalapeño: the best-known chili pepper. Hot, conical in shape, and red or green in color, it is sold fresh, pickled, or canned.
Pasilla: fresh peppers are brown and the dried ones almost black. Spicy but mild by Mexican standards, it lends flavor and color to sauces and other dishes. The fresh peppers are uncommon outside Mexico.
Poblano: similar to a small, green bell pepper with mild flavor. Available fresh, it can be stuffed or roasted.
Serrano: a fairly fiery, long, dark green chili pepper available fresh or canned. It can be finely chopped and used in sauces and vegetable dishes.

Chocolate: Mexicans blend cocoa powder with sugar and cinnamon and sometimes other flavoring ingredients – such as ground almonds – and press the mixture into disks of varying sizes. These are then dissolved in water and sometimes mixed with milk. See also page 101.

Chorizo: spicy sausage seasoned with paprika, a Spanish speciality and a legacy of the conquistadors.

Clarified butter: unsalted butter that has been melted to evaporate most of the water and separate the milk solids. The clear (clarified) butter is poured off the milky residue. Because the milk solids have been removed, the butter can be fried at higher temperatures.

Comal: a clay griddle on which tortillas are traditionally cooked.

Comida: lunch, eaten in Mexico in the early afternoon. The most important meal of the day, it consists of several courses.

Zucchini: see Calabacitas.

Crema and Jocoque: two types of thick cream, which can be replaced by heavy cream and sour cream respectively.

Desayuno: an early breakfast consisting of coffee or tea with a cake or cookies.

Epazote: a Mexican herb used to brew tea and to season a variety of dishes. Lemon balm is a good substitute. See also page 69.

Frijoles: dried beans, of which there is a huge variety in Mexico. Refried beans are a typical dish.

Guayaba: guava, a tropical fruit. Guavas are almost pear-shaped, but rounder and smaller and very strongly fragrant. They are used in Mexico for making compotes and jam.

Huachinango: red snapper. In Mexico it comes from the Gulf of Mexico and is prepared in many different ways.

Jitomate: red tomato. However, in Mexican cuisine, small little green tomatoes, called tomatillos, are widely used.

Maíze: corn. Cultivated in Mexico for thousands of years, it is still the country's staple food. It is used as corn-on-the cob, sweetcorn kernels, masa (see below), and cornmeal. See also page 84.

Mango: vitamin-rich fruit with bright yellow, juicy flesh. The pit is hard to separate from the flesh; it is long and covered in fibers.

Manteca de cerdo: rendered pork fat, a legacy of the Spanish conquistadors. Its characteristic flavor is essential for many dishes.

Margarita: famous cocktail, made with lime juice, tequila, and orange liqueur. The rims of the cocktail glasses must be briefly dipped in water and them in a bowl of salt. Loose grains of salt can be removed by lightly tapping the glass. Margaritas are served with crushed ice.

Masa: literally, the Mexican word for dough, masa is the traditional cornmeal dough from which tortillas, tamales, and atole are made. Masa is made with dried grains of corn which have been soaked in a lime and water solution, husked, and ground. Masa harina is all-purpose flourmade from dried masa.

Merienda: light, between-meals snack, equivalent to afternoon tea.

Mole: a thick spicy sauce, usually made with chili peppers, served hot. There are many variations, the most famous being *mole poblano*, made with chocolate.

Nopales: the leaves of the prickly pear cactus, which are served as a vegetable or salad ingredient. They taste rather like green beans. Available pickled in cans or jars from specialty food stores. See also Note, page 44.

Papaya: tropical fruit with yellow-red flesh, served in salads or on its own.

Pepitas: pumpkin seeds, ground with or without the shells, an ingredient in moles.

Piloncillo: unrefined, pressed brown sugar with a spicy taste. It is an essential ingredient of Café de olla. Barbados brown sugar is a good substitute.

Piña: pineapple. Commonly eaten for breakfast in Mexico – where they grow in large plantations. Pineapple is also used in salads, in meat and poultry dishes and, of course, in desserts. Although the flesh contains many important minerals and vitamins, it is unwise to eat too much pineapple at once, since pineapple contains an enzyme called bromelin, which is a meat tenderizer and can also "tenderize" the skin of your mouth! The same enzyme "eats" protein in gelatin, so you cannot make a gelatin dessert from raw pineapple. The enzyme is destroyed in cooking and canning.

Plátano: plantain. Larger, and with a blander flavor than the banana, to which it is related, this vegetable must be cooked to make it palatable, hence its alternative name of "cooking banana." Slightly under-ripe bananas can be substituted.

Pulque: the fermented, mildly alcoholic must of agave sap, unique to Mexico.

Queso añejo: very dry, mature cheese, which is used grated. Parmesan cheese is a good substitute.

Queso asadero: mild goat cheese, not widely available. Mozzarella can be used instead.

Queso fresco: crumbly cream cheese, good sprinkled over tacos, soups, and vegetables. It can be replaced by feta, Greek ewe's milk cheese.

Queso chihuahua: mild cheese not widely available. Gouda or Cheddar are good substitutes.

Queso panela: a crumbly cream cheese not widely available outside Mexico. Mozzarella cheese can be used instead.

Salsa: the Mexican name for a sauce, served with practically every dish.

Sangría: famously refreshing fruit and wine punch, particular good in summer, served ice-cold.

Sangrita: delicious fiery drink, made with tomato juice and orange juice, generously seasoned with cayenne pepper.

Sopa seca: dry soup, the name given in Mexico to the course served between the appetizer and the entrée. Sopa seca usually consists of rice, but it can also be a pasta dish.

Sweet potato: see Camote.

Tacos: stuffed and rolled-up tortillas.

Tamales: small portions of filling wrapped in a dough made from masa harina. The tamales are wrapped in banana leaves or corn husks, and then steamed. Tamales may be either sweet or savory, and are mainly served on festive occasions. Banana leaves and dried corn husks are available from specialty food stores. See also recipe, page 34.

Tejote: fruit popular in Mexico, which resembles a small, golden-yellow apple in taste and appearance.

Tequila: Mexico's most famous and popular drink. Tequila is produced from the fermentation of the sap of cactus-like plants belonging to the agave family. It is traditionally drunk with salt and lime or lemon. The most usual method is to have the serving glass rimmed with salt and serve the drink with wedges of lime. Alternatively, you can place a little salt in the hollow between your thumb and index finger, bite into the lime, take a lick of salt, then drink the tequila.

Tequila Sunrise: a popular cocktail made from tequila, lemon, and orange juice, finished with a few drops of grenadine.

Tomatillo: this looks like a small green tomato surrounded by a very thin, parchment-like husk. They are also known as green tomatoes, though they are not real tomatoes but come from the same family as the Cape gooseberry. They are native to Mexico, where they are always used fresh and unpeeled. In the U.S., you can sometimes buy them fresh; they are also available canned from specialty food stores. See also page 78.

Tortas: sandwiches with varied fillings, sold at small torta stalls.

Tortillas: thin pancakes made from cornmeal or wheat flour. You can make your own or buy them ready-made in specialty stores or larger supermarkets. If making your own, it is worth preparing a large quantity and freezing them.

Tostada: a fried tortilla, on which food is piled, as if on a plate.

Vanilla: essential flavoring for desserts. Originally cultivated by the inhabitants of Mexico and Central America, it is now produced in the south of Mexico.

Vanilla sugar is a flavored sugar which can be made at home. Place a vanilla pod in a jar of superfine sugar, close tightly, and leave for a few weeks.

CONVERSION CHART

These figures are not exact equivalents, but have been rounded up or down slightly to make measuring easier.

Weight Equivalents

Metric	Imperial
15 g	½ oz.
30 g	1 oz.
60 g	2 oz.
90 g	3 oz.
125 g	¼ lb.
150 g	5 oz.
200 g	7 oz.
250 g	½ lb.
350 g	¾ lb.
500 g	1 lb.
1 kg	2 to 2¼ lb.

Volume Equivalents

Metric	Imperial
8 cl	3 fl. oz.
12,5 cl	4 fl. oz.
15 cl	½ cup
17,5 cl	6 fl. oz.
25 cl	8 fl. oz.
30 cl	1 cup
35 cl	12 fl. oz.
45 cl	1½ cups
50 cl	16 fl. oz.
60 cl	2 cups
1 liter	35 fl. oz.

Recipe Index

Cover: Chicken and Avocado Soup (recipe, page 63) flavored with cilantro, makes a delicious, refreshing prelude to a traditional Mexican feast of wheat tortillas filled with a spicy stuffing of zucchini, sweetcorn, onion, carrot, bell pepper, and kidney beans (recipe, page 31). A glass of tequila – typically drunk with a dash of lime and salt – makes the perfect accompaniment.

Published in the United States by
Thunder Bay Press
An imprint of the Advantage Publishers Group
5880 Oberlin Drive
San Diego, CA 92121-4794
www.advantagebooksonline.com

Published originally under the title
Küchen der Welt: Mexiko

American adaptation by Josephine Bacon, American Pie, London.

ISBN 1-57145-258-3
Library of Congress Cataloging-in-Publication Data available upon request.

1 2 3 4 5 00 01 02 03 04

GRÄFE UND UNZER

EDITORS: Dr. Stephanie von Werz-Kovacs and Birgit Rademacker
Editor-in-Chief: Angela Hermann
Recipes tested by: Renate Neis
Designer: Konstantin Kern
Production: Esta Denroche
Cartography: Huber, Munich

NORTH AMERICAN EDITION:
Managing Editor: JoAnn Padgett
Project Editor: Elizabeth McNulty

Julia Fernández was born in 1951 in Mexico City, where her parents still run a thriving family restaurant. An early familiarity with the culinary specialties of her native country led to her becoming an enthusiastic cook. For this book she has put together a collection of her favorite traditional recipes. Fernández first studied German in Mexico, where she met her partner; they now live in Munich.

Michael Brauner, who photographed the food for this volume, is a graduate of the Berlin Fotoschule. He worked as an assistant to several French and German photographers before setting up on his own studio in 1984. He now divides his time between his studios in Munich, Karlsruhe and Gordes in Provence.

Marcus Langer has been a freelance graphic designer and illustrator since 1988, working for publishers and advertising agencies. Mexico has always been one of his favorite places, and his enthusiasm for the vitality and lifestyle of Latin America are reflected in the lino-cuts that he has created for this book.

Picture Credits

Color illustrations: Marcus Langer

All photographs by Michael Brauner, Food Fotografie, unless indicated below:

Cover: Graham Kirk, London. 4 to left (women at a market stall, Yucatán) and top right (pyramid at Uxmal): Bildagentur J. Dziemballa, G. Lahr; bottom left (cover near Tulum, Yucatán): Martin Thomas; bottom right (peasant and oxcart, Puebla): Bildagentur J. Dziemballa, G. Lahr. 5 top (dancer at a fiesta, Mérida): Martin Thomas: buttom (sundancer, Monte Albán): Bildagentur J. Dziemballa, Andreas M. Gross; center (cactuses, Baja California peninsula): Thomas Stankiewitz. 89 (dancer at a fiesta, Oaxaca). 10, 11 (2), 12 (2): Bildagentur J. Dziemballa, Andreas M. Gross. 13, 14: Bildagentur J. Dziemballa, Dr. Janicke. 15: Bildagentur J. Dziemballa, Andreas M. Gross. 16: Bildagentur J. Dziemballa, G. Lahr, 17 (2). 18 (2): Bildagentur J. Dziemballa, Andreas M. Gross. 19: Bildagentur J. Dziemballa, Dr. Janicke. 2021: Bildagentur J. Dziemballa, Andreas M. Gross. 21: Silvestris Fotoservice, Kastl. 22, 23 (2). 84: Bildagentur J. Dziemballa, Andreas M. Gross.

The authors would also like to thank the following for generously supplying Mexican foods:

La Tortilla, Achentalstrasse 10, 81671 Munich.
Mexico-Haus GmbH, Import-Export, Wichmannstrasse 4, 22607 Hamburg.

Color reproduction by Fotolito Longo, Bolzano, Italy
Typeset by Satz + Litho Sporer KG, Augsburg, Germany
Printed and bound by Artes Gráficas Toledo S.A.U.
D.L. TO: 247-2000